Learning with Puppets

DAVID CURRELL

Publishers   PLAYS, INC.   Boston

Published 1980 by Ward Lock Educational, London

First U.S. edition published by PLAYS, INC. 1980

Library of Congress Cataloging in Publication Data

Currell, David.
  Learning with puppets.

  Includes index.
  1. Puppets and puppet-plays in education.
I. Moore, Richard. II. Title.
PN1979.E4C79 1980   791.5'3   80-19745
ISBN 0-8238-0250-7

Printed in the United States of America

Contents

4

Part three
PRESENTATION TECHNIQUES   120

Part four
DEVELOPING PUPPETRY ACTIVITIES   162

Part five
PUPPETRY RESOURCES   186

6

Introduction

Puppetry occupies a strangely dichotomous position in our culture: it is highly popular, but often lowly regarded; it can be a serious art form, but is more often a child's pastime; it is a performance art, but has long remained fixed at the level of a craft activity. In the educational context, its power and appeal are recognized but its potential seldom realized.

The traditions of puppet theatre date back some four thousand years and there is evidence that in some areas it even preceded the drama with human actors. It is possible to identify the influence of puppet theatre on the traditional dance and drama forms of many countries, particularly in the East where puppetry continues to be regarded as a serious performance art. In the West, artists like Molière, Cocteau, Klee, Shaw, Mozart, Goethe and Craig, all took a serious interest in puppet theatre. Nevertheless, the image conjured up by the term 'puppet' has long been that of a rather trivial activity for young children.

To a large extent the world of puppet theatre is itself responsible for this image. For many centuries puppet theatre was an adult art form. Only in the nineteenth century did it become a children's entertainment and since then, the emphasis has been increasingly on puppetry as a craft activity; the performance aspect has been generally neglected. Today, however, there is renewed recognition of the need to pay attention to the performance, and the status and standards of puppet theatre are rising accordingly.

In many respects puppetry in education has reflected trends in puppet theatre itself. Puppetry in education, like puppetry in other spheres, has suffered over-emphasis of the craft aspect (reinforced in the field of education by teacher inhibition and inadequacy in the areas of drama and movement generally). It has also suffered the effects of certain 'informal' methods (as distinct from genuinely child-centred teaching approaches) which failed to provide a challenging education and instead, promoted vagueness and lack of purpose. This was reflected in puppetry activities and reinforced the trivial image of puppet theatre.

By contrast, the really child-centred approach has always looked closely at the needs and interests of the child, emotionally, socially and intellectually, and has examined the activities provided to determine how such provision meets the needs of the child and furthers his development. This approach is developing as child-centred methods become more widely understood and as less structured methods are scrutinized in the current wave of concern about education. In line with such developments, a new, more questioning approach to educational puppetry has emerged: justifications are being sought; the skills acquired, concepts developed, language possibilities, and methods of integration with other subjects are among the areas now being examined more closely than ever. Out of this an enlightened attitude to puppetry has emerged over the past few years among some teachers who not only acknowledge the power and appeal of the puppet but are making exciting explorations to maximize its potential in every area and at all levels of education.

Part one
PUPPETRY IN EDUCATION

Puppetry and learning experiences

The role of experience in learning is now generally recognized. Young children are seen as active explorers of their environment who come to know and understand objects and events initially through practical activities. Learning takes place through the interaction of two processes known as *accommodation* and *assimilation*. Accommodation takes place when one meets a concept, idea, situation or event which does not fit into one's existing mental structures so that those structures have to be modified to accommodate the new knowledge or experience; assimilation occurs when experiences fit in with existing mental structures, so that the object or event can be treated similarly to previous experiences and the existing structures are reinforced. Accommodation therefore concerns the modification and extension of understanding, while assimilation is in effect rehearsal or practice. The two processes are inextricably linked and any experience will contain elements of both, though the degree of each may vary.

If we are to introduce puppetry into the school curriculum, we must consider what experiences of this sort it provides and what educational benefits can be drawn from it. It should be made clear from the start that it is not suggested that maths, history, geography, science, etc. be *taught* through puppetry, which is a popular misunderstanding. Rather it is a matter of puppetry providing the child with opportunities to meet and understand a wide range of concepts, knowledge, skills and situations. Sometimes the child will meet a concept or situation for the first time through a puppet activity, and will have to accommodate, so that puppetry becomes a stimulus for further learning: at other times puppetry provides the opportunity to confront concepts already encountered, so providing practice and reinforcement—that is, opportunities for assimilation.

Puppetry therefore provides a stimulus for, and consolidation of, learning. Moreover, the learning that takes place is linked to a meaningful activity and is not just another of the apparently pointless exercises with which children are faced in school all too frequently. For example, the child who has to measure accurately to make two legs the same length can see more point in this activity than in simply measuring the lengths of lines in a text book to no obvious purpose. Part One of the book elaborates such possibilities for utilizing puppetry as a learning resource; Parts Two and Three discuss construction and staging techniques in detail; Part Four gives examples of educational projects using puppetry and Part Five lists various resources useful to the teacher.

It is worth noting first that puppetry is a language, a means of communicating ideas and feelings; it has a place alongside other forms of communication, whether prose, poetry, graphic arts or performance arts. If the child is to communicate as effectively as possible whatever he wishes to communicate, he needs to be initiated into these various forms of language so that he understands and appreciates each of them and can select whichever he considers most appropriate for the occasion. He may choose to beat a rhythm, perform a dance, write a story or poem, paint a picture, make a model or to give a puppet 'performance'. Some children will take more to one medium, some to another; some may choose to use puppets often, while others will never use them, though this is rare. It is important, however, that all children have access to these various forms of expression and know something about them so that they can make an informed choice. Furthermore, understanding in each of these areas serves to enrich understanding and awareness in all the rest.

While puppetry takes its place alongside other forms of creative expression, it also incorporates them and so provides a tremendous range of learning activities. It is difficult to think of an art and craft form or performance art that has not been drawn upon by puppet theatre. Through the art and craft activities which contribute to the construction of puppets, scenery and props, the child is able to meet and develop a wide range of skills and to handle and come to terms with all manner of materials and their properties, whether paper, card, fabrics, adhesives and other common craft materials, or the waste materials and containers used for instant puppets.

Such activities present many opportunities for introducing and using a variety of concepts, and the language of shape, texture, and size, comparisons, measurement and so on. Many teachers, however, would point out that their pupils have such art and craft experiences anyway. They paint pictures, make models, sew fabrics, etc. and benefit from just the sorts of learning possibilities set out here, so why do they need puppetry? The answer rests in all the opportunities for extending the experiences once the 'models' (i.e. puppets) have been made. What usually happens to a child's picture after he has painted it, or to his model after he has made it? Is it displayed in the classroom or perhaps taken home to mum? The good, sensitive teacher may get more mileage out of it in terms of language—things to discuss, ideas to follow up and develop—but there is a limit to its potential. When the model made is a puppet and the picture painted or fabric dyed is the backcloth, these are no longer items to be pinned on a board, simply to be displayed or taken home and soon forgotten. They are to be *used*. When the child has made his puppet he has only just begun to delve into the possibilities of what he has made. The experiences of his art and craft activities are now opened up and the whole realm of performance arts, together with many other aspects of the school curriculum, are drawn in.

It will be seen in the following pages that puppetry is an excellent medium for integrating a wide spectrum of the curriculum, not only crafts and performance arts but academic subjects as well. Concepts and knowledge from various areas arise frequently and may be dealt with in passing or taken up at another time. The integration has to come about naturally and has to be sensitively handled, the teacher building upon the child's initiatives and carefully planning other interventions in which she challenges, questions, provokes discussion or draws attention to relevant features of a situation.

Puppetry also performs a useful function as an integrating medium by bringing together children of varied interests, abilities and talents in a way that few other school activities can. There are so many elements in a puppet performance that there is something for everybody to do, whatever their interests or abilities. This applies at all levels in education but has been found of particular value for older children as an after-school activity compensating for the school-time trend of 'setting' children in ability groups.

A major feature of puppetry work is that it should always be a challenge, whether physical, technical or intellectual. Too often children of ten are still making the same sorts of puppet and performing the same sort of show as they did when they were seven; the challenge is missing and so it becomes 'sissy' or 'kid's stuff', even for ten-year-olds, let alone for older children. Yet there *can* always be a challenge in puppetry that is within a child's reach; when it ceases to be a challenge, it deserves not to be taken seriously.

The discussion of puppetry in education that follows does not make sharp distinctions between different age levels because the fundamental principles hold throughout the whole educational range. The actual concepts handled or techniques used may vary in complexity or in the depth to which they are developed, but the ways in which puppet theatre permeates the curriculum and offers possibilities for learning in many areas are basically the same, whatever the level. Moreover, individual differences, the tremendous range of ability found within any age group and the consequent overlap between age groups make such distinctions unhelpful.

Puppetry and language development

For too long the role of puppetry in language development has been seen simply as helping to release children's inhibitions and encourage them to talk. *Puppetry promotes language development* has become almost a slogan, as though simply 'doing puppetry' is all that is needed. This reflects a very limited view of the nature of language development and a failure to maximize the potential of puppetry in this area.

Certainly, puppetry activities encourage children who are normally reluctant to do so to talk. Paula, a six-year-old of Algerian origin, had never been heard to talk aloud in the classroom. She would sometimes talk at length with the teacher but always in a whisper, never out loud. A student on teaching practice at the school arranged for a professional puppet show to be presented one afternoon, to be followed the next morning by a classroom puppet workshop which she was conducting herself. After the show the children were reminded of what odds and ends to try to bring the next day (but the student was well-prepared in case nothing arrived from home). The following morning they arrived with their collections which were quickly sorted into appropriate containers for communal use; the workshop commenced after a brief demonstration which identified ways of setting about the work and exploring the possibilities of the materials. The need to make something fairly quickly was emphasised in order to allow plenty of time for the performance.

The children pressed ahead with their puppets and, after about twenty minutes or so, Paula quietly moved unnoticed behind a small table-top screen that had been erected on one side of the room. Suddenly everybody present was taken by surprise as a puppet with cheesebox head, decorated with tinfoil and paper doilies, popped up over the screen and in a loud voice said: 'Hello, I'm the Queen of Spain.' This was the moment that Paula needed support—help to sustain something with the puppet and not dry up: 'What are you doing here then?' She was asked. 'Oh, I'm on holiday with my husband and my family.' 'Where is your husband?' 'He's not finished yet.' The conversation continued in this way and in a few minutes Paula was reading things from displays around the room. She was reading aloud and confidently, in spite of the odd mistake—at least the puppet was and Paula corrected her: 'No, that doesn't make sense; look at it carefully and try again.' And the puppet did so.

This is a fairly concrete example of the benefits of puppetry which illustrates the point that, if the child is to talk, he must have something about which to talk, something he wants to say. The appeal of puppet activities and the performance provide a subject and the motivation to talk, but language development with puppets goes further than this. From the moment the child starts to make his puppet, language opportunities emerge.

The teacher must identify and develop such possibilities, at a level appropriate to the children concerned. With some she will be introducing words like *rough, coarse, smooth, stretchy, sticky, tacky, damp, moist,* and through discussions and questions (e.g. *What does it feel like? Is it rough or smooth?*) she gives the children the chance to use such words in context. She endeavours to get them to use the words back to her in their replies and extends the discussion, so helping the children to understand the words and incorporate them into their active vocabularies—the words they *use* rather than those they simply understand.

With others the language may centre around a problem: how to get certain materials to adhere, how to restrict a joint so that it bends in only one way, or whether there is enough of a particular material for a certain number of puppets. A child may say he wants his puppet to have a big nose; the teacher attempts to get the child to refine his concept of 'big', which is a very imprecise term: Big in what way? Does he mean long and fat, long and slim, long and pointed, fat and stubby, etc.? She may also use examples to help to clarify the terms she is using and she will not simply make a statement or ask the sort of question to which the child's answer will be only 'Yes'. She needs to structure the interaction so that the child is required to *think* about what she is saying and reply using the language which is being fostered. The example just cited asked the child to think about what he meant by 'big' on this occasion, make a decision and use the appropriate words in response; it also brought to his attention that there are different sorts of 'big' and told him, indirectly, that such a term is not very specific and that we have to use more precise terms if we are to communicate our ideas effectively to each other.

Throughout the puppet making activity such possibilities will emerge, usually springing from children's comments, questions and problems, but the teacher may also take the initiative as she spots other opportunities. Apart from the physical properties of the puppets and their construction, there is the question of character—this may mean discussing ways of achieving certain characteristics planned in advance, or exploring the characteristics a puppet appears to have after it has been constructed. How can he be made to look *menacing* (another new word)? What makes him look old? Physical characteristics, facial features, costume, hair style, movement, quality of voice and what the puppet says, all contribute to the impression created. All provide a wealth of language experiences. Here the exchange of ideas between children and between children and teacher are both valuable. This leads, of course, to the 'performance', however modest or grand, and involves not only the language of the performance but also the discussion that centres around it—the *scenario* or outline of the story (in effect, a précis), trying ideas and examining them: Is that the way a man would behave if he met the Queen? Would he be lively and mischievous, or more subdued and respectful? . . . In that case, how do you think he would speak to her? . . . Is there anything else we ought to know before this happens in the story? Where could you introduce it? (i.e. sequencing in story telling, identifying the climax, etc.)

The emphasis so far has been on the oral aspects of language as this is least well understood and utilized in puppetry in education. But, of course, there are also many opportunities for written work and reading. Keeping a record of the project and its progress, outlining the story or ideas for scenes, listing the scenes and characters needed, the scenery and props, sound effects and cues, recording lighting plans and writing programmes, are among the possibilities presented and it is writing for a purpose.

For reading too, there is benefit to be drawn from the motivation of the puppet activity which creates a need to read and a wish to read, at the same time diverting the child's attention from the anxiety of reading, teaching to a strength rather than to a problem. One class of six-year-olds visited the Puppet Centre for a workshop session to start a puppetry project; during the workshop the teacher took coloured photographs of the work in progress and the results. She then kept a similar record of the follow-up work back in school and of the performance that resulted. Children wrote their accounts of the project, then selections from the writings were matched to appropriate photographs, so that booklets were built up telling the story of 'Our visit to the Puppet Centre', 'Our puppet project in school' and 'Our puppet performance', the final booklet telling the story performed as well as showing what went on behind the scenes.

Three versions of each of the three booklets were prepared from the children's work so that the set was available at different reading levels. The size of text was varied by the use of Letraset and typescript (but it could have been written by the teacher) and the local educational resource centre made a few Xerox copies in colour. These were then bound with a comb-binding and stiff cover and the booklets gave considerable pleasure and valuable reading experience to the children concerned who took a delight in these personally relevant booklets.

Possibilities such as this will arise throughout the whole of a puppetry activity. Many more examples will be evident in the following sections which deal with other curriculum areas and the performance, because 'language development' is not a separate subject but something which goes on all the time in all areas of the child's work.

Second language teaching with puppets

While there are many distinctive techniques applied in second language teaching—whether English as a foreign language (i.e. for immigrant children) or foreign language teaching for English-speaking children—the value of puppetry in this area is generally very similar to its value in normal language development. It will not therefore be dealt with in any great detail here.

The example of Paula cited above (she was one of a class of children with language difficulties of one sort or another—there were only two English children in the class), demonstrates some of the most significant benefits of puppetry in learning a second language. It gives the child something to talk about and the motivation to talk, helping to overcome inhibitions about speaking in a foreign language. In addition to providing opportunities for language and concept development, it encourages interaction and co-operation with other children.

Art and craft in puppet theatre

The range of arts and crafts and their attendant skills involved in puppet theatre is vast. The making of puppets and props involves cutting, drawing, painting, sewing, gluing, sawing, modelling from a range of materials, sculpting or carving from wood, balsa, foam rubber, poly-styrene, casting in various materials. Even pottery puppets have been made—in the form of small pinch pots strung together to form marionettes that clinked and jangled as they moved.

Backdrops and sets offer scope for large three-dimensional modelling, two dimensional collage, scene painting and dyeing techniques, while stage construction involves woodwork and sewing. These techniques are discussed in detail in the technical section of the book.

Mathematical concepts

Construction of puppets and stages incorporates activities such as measuring, sorting, classifying and matching, dealing with shape, proportions, weight, various kinds of calculations, comparisons such as taller and shorter, stouter and slimmer, heavier and lighter, calculating sight lines and viewing angles, making designs and scale drawings, plans and elevations.

Moreover, many concepts that might not arise during construction will arise in the performance—time and space, relationships such as distance and proximity, etc. Possibilities emerge all the time; sometimes children will be handling naturally and using in a practical situation concepts met elsewhere; other concepts they may be meeting for the first time and the teacher will need to be alert to spot opportunities to develop them.

Moral development

In any performance the performer, in depicting the situation or experiences of somebody else, whether real or fictitious, has to *decentre* to some degree (i.e. move from an egocentric view of the world and try to appreciate another's point of view, feelings, etc.). This is closely related to moral development for, until the child begins to decentre, his egocentric view of events makes moral judgments very difficult to make. However, in puppetry experiences, just as in other areas of a young child's 'play', it is possible to recognize a growing feeling for such judgments before the child can actually articulate them. That is, one can see explorations of motives and consequences emerging through the interactions in which the puppets engage, before the child is able to describe or discuss them.

Moreover, because it is the puppet character who is involved and not the child directly as actor, it is sometimes easier in the early stages for the child to think and talk about what the character did. It is not always so easy to get him to articulate such an objective view when he himself has been the character. Such discussions can be very profitable at any level, whatever the age of the child, and this sort of exercise need not be limited to what emerges by chance from a performance. It may be that certain dramatic exercises are introduced which set out to explore relationships, roles, others' points of view and the like. Take, for example, a version of Cinderella in which a tiny mouse is turned into a horse to draw the carriage to the ball. He returns home after midnight having been gone some hours, then on disappearing down his hole is confronted by his wife who demands to know where he has been. How does he explain his absence? How might his wife react? What might be the outcome?

Consider now the relationship between Cinderella and her sisters, but from a rather different angle from the usual. Here we find a very attractive girl who has all the young men chasing her and who also knows how to win sympathy by playing on how overworked she is; meanwhile her poor sisters who are not nearly as young or attractive just want a chance to go to the ball without being eclipsed by their sister who always spoils everything for them. Yet again she steals the limelight. Are her sisters so unreasonable? And what must it be like to be an ugly sister? Any well known story can provide numerous such elements to explore and even quite old school-children enjoy subjecting popular themes to this sort of treatment, for which puppet theatre often seems to be a very appropriate medium.

It must be emphasized that no mention has been made of 'using puppets to teach morals'. This dubious but not uncommon activity is a contradiction in itself; it might serve to indoctrinate or encourage conformity or compliance, but that is not the same as promoting moral development. Moral judgments depend on rational decisions which take into account the weight of different arguments and which is in the common good. By contrast, the 'puppets to teach morals' movement, in which performances with a message are presented *to* children instead of *by* children, seems to depend on the power of the puppet to convince. Here the child's judgments end up appealing to what the puppet said, which is not the best way to encourage the development of a rational, morally aware person. The value of puppets in the development of moral awareness rests in the opportunities they present for decentring, examining experiences and events with some degree of feeling for, and understanding of, others, recreating past experiences and exploring familiar situations from different points of view, with the time to reflect upon and discuss these experiences after the dramatic activity. It is essential that the activity should relate to that which the children have experienced and can comprehend, for it has to be meaningful and relevant to them. It is in the child's hand that the puppets are most valuable.

Environmental studies

The elements of environmental studies involved in puppet theatre are connected with the moral development discussed in the previous section. Here too, the child is trying to understand others and their ways of life, perhaps close to home, perhaps in places further afield, in past or present times—even in terms of speculations about the future. It must be understood, however, that the reason for such elements of the curriculum is not so much to build up a store of facts, often unrelated and not particularly meaningful, but to move towards the development of an autonomous person, capable of exercising an independence of mind and action based on reason. Although knowledge is important, in some ways it is not as important as learning how to find and handle knowledge, how to ask relevant and searching questions, or learning where to look and how to look. At the same time, the child will be accommodating new knowledge to his existing mental schemes. The child learns to do this through the first-hand experience of using meaningful knowledge finding out 'for himself', with appropriate teacher intervention and guidance.

The concern here is therefore with the ways in which puppet theatre can promote such personal research, not with using puppets to convey knowledge to children, the value of which is highly questionable. Dressing a puppet or painting a scene involves considering the character, who he is, the time and place and so on. Elements of the story might require knowledge of ancient Egypt, Elizabethan England, the American Civil War, life in very hot or cold countries, or perhaps the work of the man who lives next door and is employed by the City Council.

Because they feel the need for such information, the children will engage enthusiastically in their 'research' and discover for themselves the pleasure and satisfaction to be derived from such an activity. The significant factor is that their activity has a purpose which means something meaningful to them. In other words, the knowledge is required for a reason and is applied in the performance. This involves not only finding information in books but exploration and careful observation of the environment, talking to people, conducting 'interviews', etc. The puppetry projects described later provide excellent examples of how puppet theatre can incorporate all these aspects of the curriculum.

Science

Opportunities for exploring scientific concepts are probably somewhat more limited than for other environmental studies but nonetheless they do arise quite frequently, both in the construction and performance of puppets.

Construction can involve *anatomy*, from simple parts of the body to bone structure for a skeleton; rod puppets may incorporate *levers* in the control, a *pivoted* head and a *counterbalance* or counterpull of some description; *balance* is important in exercising effective control over a rod puppet and in creating built-in movement in a marionette, for which the *centre of gravity* is a significant feature. In many ways control of the marionette is based on a *pendulum* principle. Curtains are often opened and closed by means of cords and *pulleys*; *shadows* occur both with shadow puppets and with the lighting of three-dimensional figures. In preparing the show, the effects required can demand exploration of *sound, electrical wiring* with batteries, switches and bulbs connected in series and parallel and various (safe) means of using and controlling mains lighting. Coloured lighting offers scope for exploring the *behaviour of light* and properties of *filters*, the *blending of colours* and the effects of coloured lighting on fabrics of various colours.

A study of shadows, for example, obviously could be substantial in itself; it can also open up other possibilities for imaginative writing and mathematical experiences (angle of light, length of shadows, sundials, etc.). For instance, two particularly able nine-year-olds at one school had explored shadow puppetry and related areas in some depth. Two coloured lights producing a double image gave rise to a discussion in which the old three-dimensional films were explained to them; they were able to relate these to children's 3-D viewers. The ensuing explorations (with red and green lights, cardboard spectacles with red and green filters and three-dimensional puppets made from wire) actually resulted in the creation of three-dimensional images—a tremendous achievement for them. Their own theorizing led them to hypothesize that similar effects might be achieved with polaroid lenses; though not as successful, these experiments were nonetheless valuable and illustrate very clearly the depth to which an area of puppet theatre may be taken, even at this age.

Movement, music and drama

The puppet drama has a somewhat different emphasis from the human drama. Though the human drama involves significant elements of movement and non-verbal communication, it is essentially a verbal art. The puppet drama, however, while it also has a major verbal content, places greater emphasis on the movement and non-verbal elements, since puppets need more action if they are going to sustain attention and interest. But both the puppet and human drama provide a means by which the child comes to terms with himself and with the realities of the physical and social world. They help him to decentre, explore feelings, motives, use and refine language. Such activities help to heighten awareness, understanding and insight.

The movement aspects of the puppet drama focus upon both variety and quality of movement, bodily awareness and space. The child explores the movement of the puppet in terms of its physical shape and character; he explores different types of movement such as fast, slow, powerful, confident, weak and gentle; he also explores the puppet's movement in relation to other figures and in the use of space. Throughout all these explorations run possibilities for meeting and handling a variety of language and concepts.

Puppetry activities also involve the child's own personal experiences in drama and movement as aspects of the puppet drama are explored and studied by groups and then translated back into the puppet theatre.

Music may be used to create mood or atmosphere as a background to the action, or it may be the stimulus for the action. The puppetry activity can encourage the child to listen to music and think about the ideas, feelings or images that it conjures up in order to find appropriate music for a performance. It might also encourage personal creation of music and its recording using some form of notation, whether the instruments involved are home-made, or school percussion instruments, recorders or strings. The evaluation aspect of such experiments is very important too, in helping to develop a receptivity to, and critical awareness of, music.

Language possibilities arise here too, even simply in the attempt to find a suitable rhythm or 'musical phrase' to be repeated as accompaniment to a puppet moving across the stage, to convey a limp, or a threatening approach. The discussion that centres around such an exercise, describing the impression intended and that which is created, can be quite remarkable and productive.

Pluto, King of the Underworld, from *The Story of the Seasons*

Puppetry for children with special needs

This section is concerned with any child with special needs, whether a child with learning or behaviour difficulties in the ordinary classroom, or a child in a special class or school, whatever the nature of his problem.

The physically handicapped child, of course, derives the same intellectual benefits from puppetry as any other child, but it often offers a bonus for children who need motivation to practise various skills requiring a manual dexterity or who need to exercise particular limbs or muscles. A child who repeatedly resisted doing his hand exercises could not be stopped once a glove puppet was on his hand and children with no arms have used their feet to make and perform simple rod puppets. Deaf and partially-hearing children have given performances of tremendous power and feeling. A puppet performance also makes it possible for any child to play any part, whatever his physical characteristics or handicap.

The power of the puppet to command attention is quite remarkable and I have seen the benefits of this clearly illustrated in puppet activities which involved autistic children. It started with a request for a performance, to which I agreed, although a little apprehensive about how the show would be received, given the nature of autism. I decided that the most appropriate type of performance would be a series of short marionette variety items which would not demand too great a concentration on any one item for a long period, and to try to encourage some form of participation by the audience, made up of less than a dozen children across a wide age range. The children's response to the performance was splendid. Some joined in very enthusiastically while those with a more severe condition turned away or hid their faces, but still peeped through their fingers or under their arms to see what was happening, which was a considerable achievement, since securing the attention or response of autistic children is not at all easy. After the performance, the children 'explored' the puppets, feeling the faces, for example, and were encouraged to relate them to their own bodies: How many eyes does it have? How many eyes do you have? Do you have two eyes too? Some children helped to pack the puppets with great care; then, over tea, they talked with the performers about what they had seen and enjoyed. Subsequent activities built upon this experience and one child, to everybody's delight, constructed his own puppet show.

Puppetry is also used fairly frequently in psychodiagnosis and psychotherapy. Unfortunately, some very disturbing trends have emerged in this area recently, with many inadequately trained and unqualified people running psychodrama or psychotherapy sessions using puppets. They fail to appreciate that puppetry is such a powerful medium that situations can be created which an unqualified leader cannot handle and does not know how to conclude satisfactorily. This is an area that should be left to the qualified specialist. It does not fall within the scope of the present work, but those engaged professionally in the field may find many aspects of this book relevant to their work.

Children with behaviour problems and learning difficulties find puppetry of great value. They often have a very poor self-image since they have experienced repeated failure or are constantly being told how dreadful their behaviour is—and, of course, it *is* dreadful at times. The child, however, comes to believe that in terms of work or behaviour, he cannot do anything right, that he has nothing to offer and is not a valued member of the community. What such children need is not people to do things for them, but the chance to do something for others. Puppetry gives them such a chance. The activity can be as simple or as complex as necessary to remain within the children's capabilities yet still provide the challenge that is vital to sustain interest and ensure the sense that something of worth has been achieved.

With puppets these children can achieve success in a very short time—a success that is recognized by their peers, their parents, their teachers and, most important, themselves. Even a little success boosts confidence and morale and often brings about a noticeable improvement in both behaviour and academic performance. In addition, as was noted in another context, benefits accrue from the motivation from puppetry for work in other curriculum areas. For such children puppetry presents a reason for the work, for they, more than other children, often have difficulty in seeing any purpose in school work.

Linda was an eight-year-old of very limited academic ability and not at all confident in her attitude. She did not seek to engage in many activities, although she would join in if encouraged. On one occasion she became involved in making some very simple shadow puppets, but at this stage it had not occurred to her that the other children might expect her to perform with her puppet. However, realizing she was expected to pull her weight and contribute to the performance, she did so even if a trifle apprehensively. Her mother had called to take her to the dentist and slipped in to wait and to see what was happening without Linda knowing (she was already behind the shadow screen). Linda's puppet was cut out quite roughly but was nonetheless effective as a shadow; she had only a little to say but she said it clearly and her mother was delighted: 'I never thought I'd ever hear her talk out like that,' she commented, then added, 'She's the bright one in our family you know—gets her brains from her dad.' This was a great boost for Linda, who had surprised herself too. She had enjoyed making a contribution that was valued and being part of a performance the other children obviously enjoyed. An immediate improvement in her confidence was noticed and she entered into various activities with a newly-discovered enthusiasm. Her academic work subsequently improved slightly, which might be attributed in part to her work with puppets. In any case, even if the puppetry had had no influence on Linda's academic performance, the benefits it brought her as a person and a personality, were unquestionable.

A group of boys in a boarding school for maladjusted children were taken to participate in a puppetry workshop. They joined in a little reluctantly at first, but they soon became thoroughly involved and afterwards all their energies were directed towards creating a puppet performance. This was a trying time for the teacher but from the frustrations, tantrums and flying tools emerged a set of puppets and a performance. The teacher had found a children's home some distance away which was eager to have a show and the boys were given the responsibility of getting themselves there, setting up, performing and returning to the school entirely on their own. They set out excitedly, and a little nervously, with their portable stage and suitcases of puppets and props. They returned to the school even more excited than they left, for the show had been a tremendous success and it led to a series of similar performances by the boys. (One enterprising boy even started trying to obtain orders for making puppets!) Now the boys had something to offer, something appreciated by others. Knowing that the group depended on the contribution of each member throughout the project, they rose to the occasion and for the first time worked together towards a common goal. Afterwards one boy said, 'Thank you,' to the teacher. It was the first time he had done so for anything and this was a real break-through.

Organizing puppetry activities

Introducing puppetry

Just where does one start? How does one introduce puppetry into the classroom? This question does not usually arise since children are exposed to a considerable amount of puppet theatre, largely on television and occasionally, but unfortunately not often, as a live performance. It needs only one or two children to suggest making puppets and the idea soon spreads. In such circumstances the teacher must decide how much attention the children concerned are likely to need and whether to start off a small group, letting others join in gradually, or whether to make it a large group or class activity.

For younger children, one would hope that a few standard puppets and materials for puppet making were available for use at any appropriate time. Where puppets and puppetry activities are always available as one of the choice of activities it does not mean they lose their natural appeal and it avoids the situation where everybody clamours to make puppets just because it is the latest fad, as so often happens with any activity offered only occasionally. Such fads are also usually short-lived. For older children, the timetable structure will often make puppetry an activity that has to be fitted into certain periods, although, with the more liberal approach found in many schools today, more possibilities for relating work in different areas of the curriculum are opening up.

At any age level, impetus may be given to puppetry activities by a live professional performance. Cost of travel in particular often makes it more viable to engage a company to perform at the school rather than go out to a theatre for a show, but there are many extra benefits to be gained from the experience of visiting a theatre and all the conventions that this involves. Whether or not the children see a performance, they need to be exposed to the possibilities of puppet theatre and particularly to the different types of puppet possible (since they often think of one particular type, depending on what is currently most popular on television), the sorts of things that puppets can do and ways of presenting them.

The teacher can demonstrate such possibilities using the puppets she should have made herself in exploring the medium before introducing it to the children, for, however much help one gets from books, attending shows or lecture-demonstrations, it does not replace the need to actually try it oneself. To cite a simple example, it is not uncommon to hear a teacher grumbling to a child using glove puppets that the puppets are disappearing: 'Keep your hands up; we can't see the puppets,' she complains. When I run teachers' courses I often let them experience what it is like to hold puppets in the air for a long time—they soon appreciate why the child's arms drop and the need for a comfortable acting level.

In presenting demonstrations of the possibilities of puppets, whether to adults or children, I follow the same basic principle: introducing a wide range of puppets which exemplify different types (and variations within types), a variety of construction materials and methods and various means of control and presentation. In the process, a few finished puppets are demonstrated, but the emphasis is upon the use of lay figures which demonstrate the possibilities without presenting something to be copied. Then a few explorations are made of materials and their possibilities; for example, one might pick a yogurt carton from a collection of 'junk' materials and ask: What would this make? A head? Which way up would you use it? What if you turn it up the other way—does it change the character? . . . What features do we need? Can you think of anything that would do for eyes? Let's try some of them. Which of these is best? Why is this button better than that bottle top? (e.g. because it catches and reflects the light and gives more life to the eyes). Now what about the nose? Ears? Floppy ears?

So the demonstration continues, looking at all aspects of the puppet, its costume, etc., quickly identifying many suitable and alternative possibilities but never completing a figure that might be taken as *the* way to do it and copied religiously. This approach, which is primarily concerned with understanding the puppet, has been found to promote much more adventurous and imaginative use of materials than the presentation of a set of finished figures.

The workshop

A puppetry workshop, whether it be a special studio or just space in a classroom, needs careful and thoughtful organization. The teacher should try to build up, with the children's help, a wide selection of attractive fabrics and trimmings (sorted according to the type of material—cottons, satins, nets and lace, fur fabric, etc.) and empty cartons and other waste materials suitable for modelling, similarly sorted. The selections can be stored in boxes of reasonable size so that they can be managed by the children and should be accessible and well displayed.

It is also essential to have a small selection of good tools appropriate to the children concerned. Some teachers, for example, are fearful of letting children handle sharp scissors, but without them the task is so much more difficult and frustrating than it need be. If the tools are set out on racks so that everything has its place, finding what one needs is an easy matter and it is also possible to see at a glance that everything has been returned at the end of the session. Good adhesives are essential for there is nothing worse than having to use glues that just will not stick the materials used; contact glues which hold and set immediately are desirable, but they are not permitted in schools in some areas.

It is advisable to assign certain areas or tables for certain types of work—e.g. gluing table, sewing table, painting table. These facilities are then accessible to children working on activities other than puppets and such an organization avoids the problems of children spilling paint or glue on the materials or having to stretch across paint pots and brushes to reach something else. The well-stocked puppet workshop also contains plenty of newspapers for covering tables; at the end of a workshop session, all that is needed is to roll up the newspapers with the rubbish inside, leaving the workshop clean.

During workshop activities the teacher will intervene to pose questions, make suggestions and answer questions—not by giving a direct answer, perhaps, but by asking further questions or bringing something to the child's attention so that he is led to see the answer for himself. It is a very good idea to put a time limit on the basic making, otherwise there is a tendency for this activity to drift on and for insufficient time to be left for performing with the puppets. This applies whether what is involved is a single session or a whole project leading to a grand performance; the construction side always takes longer than one thinks unless one is very strict about it. Even many professional puppeteers are notorious for still making their puppets a matter of hours before the first performance and not giving sufficient time to rehearsals.

To give some idea of the timing of such work: a workshop session could begin with a time limit of just thirty minutes for making a puppet and perhaps a few minutes extra at the end for rounding off the construction. The group could then have a short time to discuss their ideas and explore the possibilities of the individual puppets. They would move quickly on from this to work on their performance—perhaps for twenty minutes. A short break at this point is useful to refresh the group, discuss problems and consider how the performance is coming together. Then back to the show, with a run through of the whole piece, and the performance is ready to be seen. Finally, time to reflect and evaluate after the performance is highly desirable. The whole activity from beginning to end might thus take an hour and three quarters, perhaps two hours if it is preceded by a short demonstration, but in this example the constructional work itself takes only a quarter of the total time needed.

For a longer project the puppet making might well take a little longer, but it must not be allowed to drag on. Most children need to see some positive results fairly quickly and methods which take weeks to finish or where children have to wait days for something to dry before going on to the next stage are frustrating and counter-productive.

The performance

It must be appreciated that a performance with puppets, in educational terms, can be anything from one or two young children sitting improvizing encounters with puppets as an element in their natural, spontaneous play, through small performances for the class, to full-scale productions for the school or parents. The benefits accruing from each type may differ slightly, but all are valuable.

The first type of use is occasionally referred to as 'dead end puppetry' but this is to misunderstand the very real benefits that flow from allowing the child to reflect on his environment in this way, as he does in other elements of his play. Moreover, a young child's level of cognitive development might make this a more appropriate activity than a formal performance at this stage. It is unfortunate, however, that many children are never extended beyond this sort of activity as they grow and develop intellectually and this is when it *does* become dead end puppetry.

Some teachers seem to work on the assumption that puppetry activities are for special occasions, always with some grand performance, perhaps an Open Day, in mind. Anybody who has really explored the possibilities of puppetry in education will know that this is a limited view and that so much is to be gained from the everyday use of puppets. It is important, however, that children do not simply make quick puppets, give a short improvized performance and leave things there. Even at the level of an everyday classroom activity there should be the time and encouragement to reflect self-critically on the activity and to develop it.

For young children it is a good idea to keep a set of strong, standard figures ready-made in the classroom. These might be a mixture of characters met in everyday life and nondescript figures which can quickly be made to represent a range of characters. There will be times when the children simply wish to use puppets, not make them, or when they need puppets for immediate use. On such an occasion the delay while they make the puppets can reduce their enthusiasm and frustrate them in their eagerness to perform. However, having used the standard figures, there is no reason why they should not be encouraged to develop the idea and make their own puppets for it.

Turning to the needs of children who are able to undertake a more structured performance, whatever the level, the two all-embracing approaches are either to make puppets with no specific performance in mind or to make puppets for a specific story. Both are valid: sometimes the motivation comes from wanting to make and use puppets, sometimes it comes from a wish to perform a story where puppetry seems the appropriate medium. When considering the educational benefits and appropriateness for different age groups, it must be remembered that these are two very different sorts of exercises—making a puppet and seeing how it turns out and how it moves, as opposed to making a puppet which successfully conveys a particular character and is able to do whatever is required of it.

Whatever the approach to a performance, one important element is the relative sizes of figures. If one child makes an elephant nine inches high and another makes a man eighteen inches high because they have not co-ordinated this feature of the work, the results can be very entertaining but they could also spoil what the children are trying to achieve. Some common agreement about the range of sizes therefore may be necessary.

Another aspect that may need co-ordination is what characters the children are to make. For example, a puppet performance is often suggested in conjunction with Hallowe'en and many teachers are surprised to find that they end up with twenty eight near-identical witches. It is quite remarkable how many Hallowe'en puppet performances centre around a witches' convention!

A scene from *The Secret of Fire*

What type of puppet?

The type of puppet used may be determined by individual preferences, the capabilities of the children, the needs of the story and the materials and time available. It has long been popularly thought that glove puppets are the most suitable type for young children and marionettes the most difficult; rod and shadow puppets have been ignored generally. However, every type of puppet can be very simple, or much more challenging.

Glove and rod puppets with their direct control are ideal for the sort of fast, robust action that young children often introduce into their stories; they also have an intimacy with the operator that particularly suits young children. Glove puppet design is limited in so far as it must contain a hand (though it can therefore pick up objects easily); the glove puppet's gestures are limited to the movement of the young operator's fingers inside the glove and it is not easy for children to make their own well-fitting, comfortable gloves, so this can easily become a teacher-orientated activity. Glove puppets therefore might be more appropriate for slightly older children.

Rod puppets, like marionettes, offer greater scope for creative design. Simple rod puppets are easy for a child to hold and move and extra rods can be added to control hands. The puppet can be given an articulated head or it can be developed as a rod-and-hand puppet, to give just a few examples of more challenging rod puppets for older children. Marionettes need not be the formidable and complex figures they are often thought to be, as is made clear in the technical section. One class of seven-year-olds made a magnificent set of fairly large 'junk-box' marionettes, taking the characters from a popular set of reading books, and the results were splendid. Marionettes also offer many opportunities for older children to demonstrate their resourcefulness and inventiveness and rod puppets and marionettes are capable of executing both simple and subtle movements with grace and charm. Marionettes, however, are unsuitable for fast, forceful action because of the method of control and the danger of tangles.

Shadow puppets are the most under-rated form of puppetry. In some ways they are not as dynamic as three-dimensional figures and the operators cannot see the actual effect they are producing so shadow puppets are not so suitable for very young children, but for others they are excellent. They are quick to make and easy to operate and a show can be ready in no time at all. They offer great scope for extending work on design, shape, texture, colour, at a level appropriate to every age group. Shadows are suitable for ordinary plays but are particularly effective for illustrating a narrated story, a mixture of narration and dialogue and as a background for three-dimensional puppets, the shadows presenting dream sequences, events recalled or distant action.

Such a mixture of puppets—glove and rod puppets, rod puppets and marionettes, or shadows and any other type—is not uncommon and the introduction of actors (often masked) with puppets is also an increasingly popular way of extending the scope of the performance.

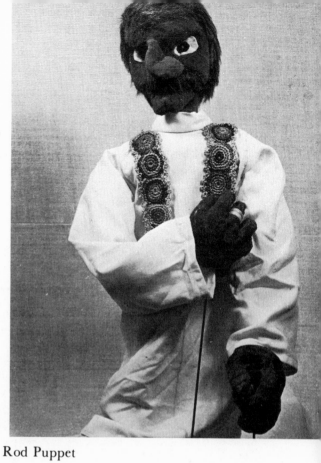

Glove puppet

Rod Puppet

Shadow puppet

Marionette

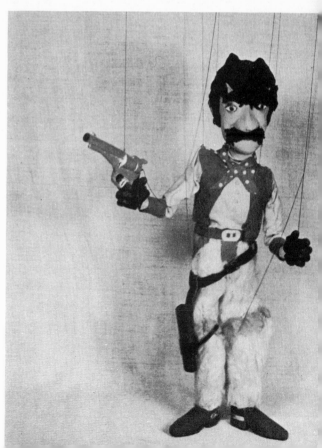

Staging

Puppets may be presented without any staging, using some form of open structure which provides acting levels with the puppeteers visible, or with a full stage or booth in which the puppeteers are hidden. The trend in puppet theatre generally is away from the conventions of a traditional stage and children might profitably be encouraged to explore a more adventurous use of space.

It should be recognized that young children will improvize staging naturally, using anything to hand, or they may use their puppets with no 'stage' of any description. In line with their intellectual development and the development of their play, they will soon come to require more realism and 'proper' staging. While they may be encouraged to be more adventurous in this respect, it is not reasonable to *expect* them to be able to grasp what is in fact a different kind of convention and to feel secure working within it. As they progress into and through the seven to eleven age range they will be able to accept, understand and cope with the less traditional methods and, from eleven or twelve, they will find open, flexible staging challenging, adaptable and well-suited to the less conventional performance styles which seem to appeal to this age group.

Further considerations determining the staging will be the type of puppet to be used, the demands of the play, the preference of the operators, the materials and particularly storage space available, for it is important that the staging does not steal valuable classroom space. The size of the staging must be considered carefully too, for this determines how many operators, and therefore characters, can be accommodated on stage at any one time. It is essential that the operators are not cramped or a back-stage battle for space might ruin the performance. Flexible, open staging, of course, does not place quite the same sort of restriction on the performance.

Developing a performance

Where children begin with a set of figures and no particular story in mind, the energy that has been invested in the construction will give way to frustration when the puppets are completed if the children or teacher do not know what to do with them. This is a crisis point in puppetry. On completion of their figures, therefore, the children can be invited to explore what they can do, their limitations and capabilities, how they move best, how they look and what more they learn about or see in the character as they use it. Then they may move into interaction with other figures, from which the drama may emerge. However, this is the stage that needs careful handling; all too well known is the situation when two characters take the stage, say hello, tell each other their names, make some other brief exchange, then dry up, whereupon the most common outcome is a recourse to aggressive action with one puppet beating the other over the head. It may be that in coming to terms with the limitations and strengths of the medium and in handling a medium in which violent action does not cause personal harm or invoke punishment, this is a natural phase through which to pass, but the teacher might need to offer support over this period or the drama might never develop.

The teacher may have only to ask about the puppets' relationship to each other, how they would greet each other therefore, what they might have to talk about, how they would feel and behave if puppet *x* came along, what *x* would be likely to do––'Well, let's see what happens then.' (It is worthy of note that two-character interactions are very different from three or more character interactions which are more profitable dramatically.) The children can provide the answers, the action and the dialogue; they need just a little help to structure their thinking. The dramatic possibilities that emerge from such explorations may then be developed into a performance or, with the knowledge that has emerged from the explorations, a story-line may be determined through discussion and then elaborated.

The alternative method of starting with a story in mind—even if it is only an outline—is for some a more immediately fruitful approach. The story can be made up on the spot, taken from a child's written story, or a story read, suggested by a television or radio programme or based upon an event in history. If they are able, the children should be encouraged to consider the suitability of the material for a puppet play: fantasy, folk tales, simple comedy, zany sketches and uncomplicated plays can be very effective but heavy drama and complex plots are not generally suitable. Besides, good stories do not always make good plays so one should consider the dramatic content and, in particular, how much of the story can be translated into action, a key to good puppet theatre.

In the educational situation it is usually preferable not to have a rigid script which is learned by heart; in work with children, this tends to lack the vitality and feeling achieved when some spontaneity and improvization are possible, and results in confusion and panic when lines are forgotten. A tape-recorded script is not a good idea either since it excludes any spontaneity and takes no account of audience reaction. It is not easy to achieve a really good recording and the taped voice lacks the power of the live voice to command and hold attention, particularly that of children. It also introduces an unnecessary element of risk in the shape of technical hitches. It should be borne in mind too that, whenever possible, the operators should speak for their own puppets; this promotes better co-ordination of movement and speech and the added identification fostered between puppet and puppeteer improves both the quality of the movement and the expressiveness of the voice. If for some reason some children are to speak while others manipulate, it is essential that the speakers can see the puppets on stage.

Though a rigid script is not recommended, for any performance some form of *scenario*, however achieved, should be arrived at: i.e. an outline of the action, detailing who does what, to whom and where. Without such a framework it is possible for the performance to go off at a complete tangent, not develop properly and not arrive at a satisfactory conclusion, with the performers simply indulging themselves and the audience bored. The scenario provides the structure within the limits of which the performers have freedom of expression and improvization: provided x does this or that to y and conveys the idea that . . . , it is up to the performer exactly how to do it or say it in keeping with the character.

The scenario provides the basis on which the characters are made and on which the performance can then be built; scenes may be tried, evaluated and developed, modified or abandoned; encounters may be acted by the children themselves, then transposed into the puppet play. It should be remembered, however, that human acting is not always a good basis for puppet acting. The children should be encouraged to bear in mind what puppets in general, and theirs in particular, can do well and the sorts of things it is better to avoid.

A golden rule with puppet theatre is to keep the play short. Most shows at any level are too long and need tightening. It will often be found too, that the smaller the puppet, the shorter the show it can sustain and the speeches it can handle successfully.

In order to build strong action, it may be found useful to have the puppets act out the story entirely in mime first and then to add whatever dialogue is necessary. The limitations of speechlessness often necessitate a deeper search into the possibilities of conveying meaning through action.

Adequate time to rehearse any show is essential but, at the same time, the rehearsals should be kept short. Even with adults, fatigue soon sets in and the value of the session rapidly diminishes. As well as serving to get the story and dialogue right, rehearsals may focus attention on the main movements and gestures of the figures and on achieving a variety of gesture within the limits of characterization. The children also need to be able to communicate which puppet is speaking, not by jerking it to every syllable of speech, but by appropriate movement and gestures, while the other figures are kept, not lifeless, but listening attentively and making subdued movements in response.

Entrances and exits often need attention too, for it is a common fault to swing the puppet on to the stage or let it pop up as if out of the ground and only then to start manipulating it. The puppet must be operated in character before it comes into view and must enter appropriately, whether through a door or arch, from behind wings or a piece of scenery, or up imaginary steps inside the booth if it has to come up from below the acting level. Otherwise the whole illusion will be destroyed.

Rehearsals are the time to get used to the need to have absolute silence back-stage during the performance and to discover how to cover, by improvization, any hitches that may arise. Checking puppets and equipment at the beginning and end of each session should become a matter of routine and everybody should know where everything belongs, for everything back-stage must have a specific place if the proceedings are to run smoothly.

In order that the puppeteers may see how the show looks to the audience, a mirror might be introduced into some rehearsals, but care should be taken that the puppeteers do not come to rely upon it. The switching of roles, so that a performer can sit out front and watch the scene he usually performs, is also very useful (and helps in case of absences), but this does not show him his own manipulation. Videocassette and videotape facilities are increasingly available in schools, and studying a recording, being able to review scenes as often as required, is invaluable to puppeteers. However, it is advisable to have a recording made with one fixed camera shooting the whole action. Extra cameras cutting to different shots, suddenly giving a close-up, etc. may be artistic and creative as 'television' but it can spice up a performance, adding dimensions that will not be present when it is presented live to an audience.

This, of course, is also the time when music, sound effects, scene-changing and lighting, if used, are perfected and when the whole back-stage choreography is worked out. What happens back-stage, how characters and puppeteers can pass each other and keep the puppets moving in character, where best to place each prop or puppet when not in use, who is going to pass what to whom, can be as important as what happens on stage.

If the performance is rehearsed as separate scenes it is essential to have adequate rehearsals of the whole show from beginning to end, to see how it looks, how it hangs together and to smooth out any problems that might emerge. It is surprising how many problems (not having time to get from point A to point B, changing scenery, reaching a different puppet and getting it on stage in time or even a breakdown in the logical development of the story) do not emerge until the play is rehearsed as a whole, however much individual scenes are rehearsed.

With the show rehearsed, the snags ironed out and all puppets and equipment carefully checked, the play is ready to be performed, but this is not the end of the activity. After the performance the children may reflect, evaluate and develop the play in the light of how it was received. They may give more performances and even prepare a sequel using the same figures. As with all areas of puppet theatre, the possibilities are boundless.

Part two
CONSTRUCTION
TECHNIQUES

A note on construction techniques

In constructing puppets, the more traditional methods may be used—and suitable techniques are described later. Generally, however, *instant puppets*, made from any materials and odds and ends that may be handy, are preferable because of the speed and cheapness of construction.

Instant puppetry techniques have been known as 'junk puppetry' but the term is going out of fashion because of its unfortunate connotations. 'Junk' not only encourages a trivial image of puppetry but creates the wrong sort of mental attitude for approaching the materials. The empty cartons and containers available to the puppeteer were designed very carefully for their original use, with considerations of size, shape, feel and the influence of the container on the shopper in mind. The puppeteer, recognizing this, should approach the materials, not as 'junk', but with a readiness to see the possibilities of shape, natural colour, etc.; in other words, his approach should be lively and imaginative, based on an exploration of, and sensitivity to, materials.

There are no hard and fast rules for constructing puppets; what is required is a flexible approach, developing the construction to suit the needs of the puppet and the materials available. Instant puppets may be used just as they are or dressed—and once they are dressed, it is hard to tell that some are made from waste materials.

Useful tools for puppet making

At the simplest level a puppet 'workshop' can function with just a pair of scissors, glue and tape, but the more tools there are available, the greater the scope for construction. The tools shown in *Figure 1* are a useful selection.

Figure 1   Selection of tools used in puppet making

36

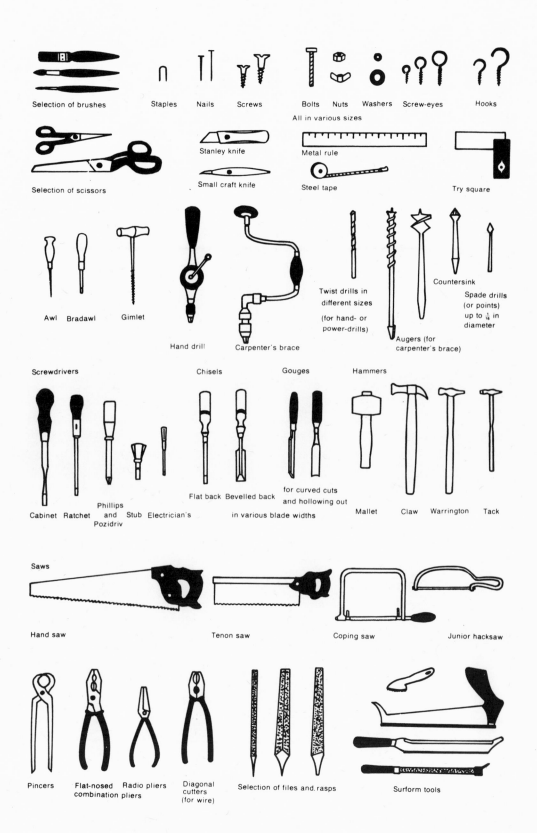

Selection of brushes

Staples

Nails

Screws

Bolts   Nuts   Washers   Screw-eyes

Hooks

All in various sizes

Selection of scissors

Stanley knife

Small craft knife

Metal rule

Steel tape

Try square

Awl   Bradawl   Gimlet

Hand drill

Carpenter's brace

Twist drills in different sizes

(for hand- or power-drills)

Countersink

Augers (for carpenter's brace)

Spade drills (or points) up to $\frac{1}{16}$ in diameter

Screwdrivers

Cabinet   Ratchet   Phillips and Pozidriv   Stub   Electrician's

Chisels

Flat back   Bevelled back

in various blade widths

Gouges

for curved cuts and hollowing out

Hammers

Mallet   Claw   Warrington   Tack

Saws

Hand saw

Tenon saw

Coping saw

Junior hacksaw

Pincers

Flat-nosed combination pliers   Radio pliers

Diagonal cutters (for wire)

Selection of files and rasps

Surform tools

37

Proportions for a puppet

Puppet proportions are usually a little different from human proportions. Head, hands and feet are usually exaggerated slightly; a puppet made to human proportions generally looks rather lanky. Approximate proportions are set out in *Figure 2* but it is important to bear in mind that it is the variation of proportions that helps to add character to the body shape and facial features and one should not be afraid to change proportions deliberately.

Common mistakes are making the puppet too tall and thin (body shape is frequently overlooked), setting the eyes too high in the head or too close together, setting the nose too low or making the chin very weak so that there is little room for the mouth. Ears too, get put in some funny positions and hands and feet are often too small.

It is useful to observe carefully the heads of various people, looking at features and proportions, comparing the length of hands against the face, comparing hands and feet, and so on. The sizes of puppet head, hands and feet relative to each other are the same as human proportions.

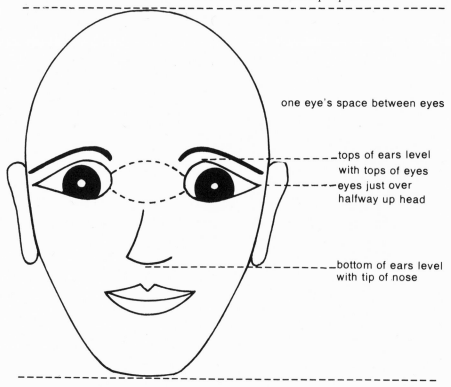

one eye's space between eyes

tops of ears level
with tops of eyes
eyes just over
halfway up head

bottom of ears level
with tip of nose

Figure 2 (a)

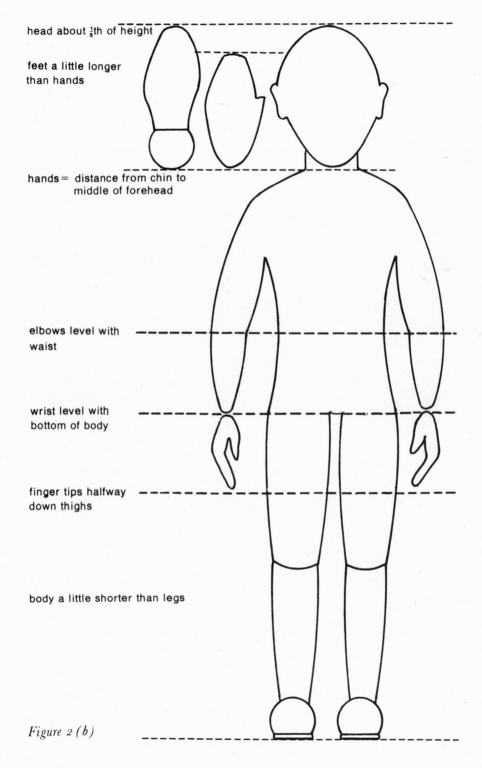

head about ⅛th of height

feet a little longer
than hands

hands = distance from chin to
middle of forehead

elbows level with
waist

wrist level with
bottom of body

finger tips halfway
down thighs

body a little shorter than legs

Figure 2 (b)

Techniques for making heads

Instant puppet techniques for making heads are described for each type of puppet under their different sections. The techniques detailed here are suitable for more complex and durable heads made by the traditional techniques of modelling, sculpting, etc. They are appropriate for all types of three-dimensional puppets.

When making the head, a number of points need to be considered:

1 The puppet maker should bear in mind the spatial relationship between puppet and maker and between puppet and audience (*see Figure 3*). At the construction stage the maker is usually looking down at the puppet but in performance the audience is often looking up at it. Therefore, the maker must take care·not to make the puppet head angled slightly upwards (a common tendency) or its focus will be way above the audience. If anything, it could be tilted *just a little* downwards, but not noticeably.

2 When making a puppet's neck, take into account the type of puppet. A glove puppet has an oval-shaped neck-opening to accommodate two fingers for manipulation; it also has a slight bell-bottom or a small ridge around the bottom to help secure the glove and prevent it slipping off the neck (*Figure 4a*). A rod puppet and marionette may have head and neck in one piece (*Figure 4b*), or a separate neck with the head pivoted on it (*Figures 4c and 4d*).

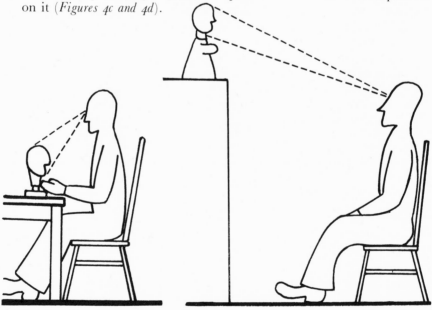

(a) Relationship of maker to puppet   (b) Relationship of puppet to audience

Figure 3

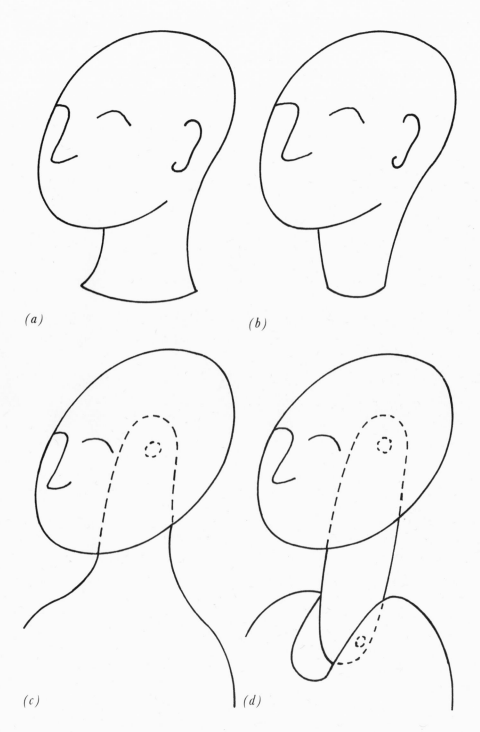

(a)

(b)

(c)

(d)

Figure 4

Sock or stockinette head

Materials: an old sock *or* piece of stockinette, fabric *or* foam rubber stuffing *or* an old ball, cardboard, a rod, thread

1   Take the sock or piece of stockinette and stuff it with the ball, pieces of fabric or foam rubber.
2   For a marionette, knot the sock and cut it off at the heel (*Figure 5a*).
3   For a glove puppet, cut off the sock at the heel, push a conical cardboard neck tube firmly into the head and glue and bind the sock securely to it (*Figure 5b*).
4   For a rod puppet, cut off the sock at the heel, push a rod into the head and glue and bind the sock securely around it (*Figure 5c*).
5   Glue or stitch on felt features, beads or buttons for eyes, etc.

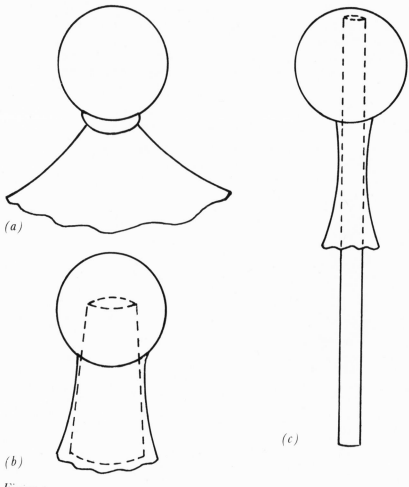

(a)

(b)

(c)

Figure 5

Plastic wood head

Materials: modelling stand, plasticine, petroleum jelly, plastic wood, acetone

1. Make a modelling stand by screwing together a block of wood and a thick dowel (*Figure 6a*).
2. Model the head in plasticine on the stand (*Figure 6b*).
3. Cut out cardboard ears and fasten them in the plasticine model.
4. Carefully smear the plasticine model all over with a little petroleum jelly (to prevent the plastic wood sticking to the plasticine) but do not smear the ears.
5. Cover the head with a layer of plastic wood, applying it in small pieces (*Figure 6c*). Dipping the plastic wood in a little acetone makes it easier to blend pieces together and gives a smoother finish.
6. When covering the ears, first smear the card with glue (UHU or Bostik No. 1) and then add the plastic wood.
7. When the plastic wood is dry, cut open the head (behind the ears and over the top of the skull) and carefully remove the plasticine (*Figure 6d*). Inspect for thin patches by holding up the skull to the light.
8. Glue the two shells together; cover the joint and any thin patches with more plastic wood.
9. Smooth the head with glasspaper and then paint it (Reeves' Polymer Paint or Rowney Acrylacolour are recommended, mixed with water for a matt finish, not the medium or the paint will dry shiny).

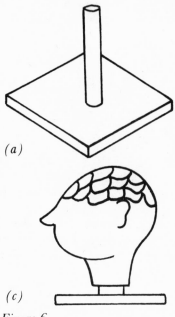

(a)

(b)

(c)

(d)

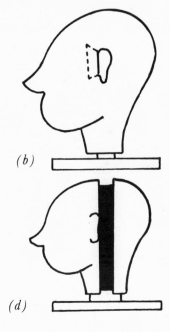

Figure 6

Paste and paper head

Materials: modelling stand, plasticine, tissue paper, paste, newspaper

1 Model the plasticine head on a modelling stand, as described in the previous example. Modelling must be deep and bold or it will disappear when the layers of paper are applied.
2 Cover the head with squares of damp tissue paper.
3 Then apply approximately one inch (25 mm) squares of newspaper, overlapping slightly, stuck down with cellular paste.
4 It is essential to allow each layer to dry before applying the next.
5 A minimum of four layers is recommended, with each layer pressed firmly onto the previous one.
6 When the head is thoroughly dry, cut it open, remove the plasticine and re-join with more paste and paper.

Figure 7 **A paste and paper head**

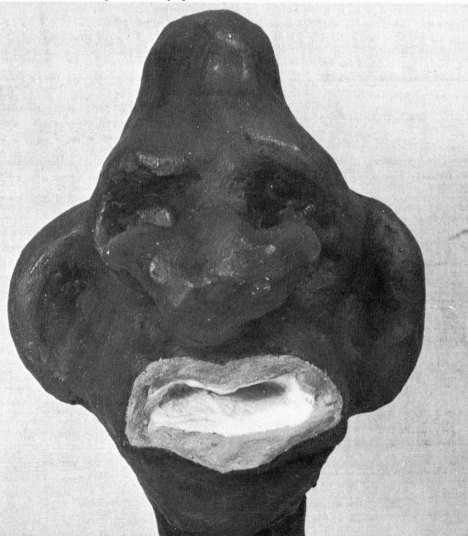

Alabastine and muslin head

Materials: modelling stand, plasticine, tissue paper, muslin (mull), Alabastine (plaster filler)

1   The technique is the same as for the paper and paste head but using squares of muslin dipped in plaster filler.
2   Three layers of muslin are recommended.
3   In order to ensure proper coverage of each layer, colour the second layer of plaster with a little paint. Any patches missed can then be seen clearly.
4   The advantage of this method is that muslin is more easily modelled around shapes than paper and each layer can be applied without waiting for the previous one to dry.

Figure 8 Alabastine and muslin heads at different stages of construction

Foam rubber head

Materials: block of foam rubber

1   Draw the full-face and profile views of the head, with or without a neck, on two sides of a block of foam rubber (*Figure 9a*), making sure there is enough space for the profile view (a common fault is to make the back of the head too square and lacking in shape because not enough foam rubber has been allowed).

2   Cut away the main pieces of waste to establish the basic shape (*Figure 9b*), then work on the detail, taking care to keep the modelling bold (*Figure 9c*).

3   Ensure that the original shape of the block is not evident when the cutting is finished (often the head is left rather square and the face flat because the cutting has not been bold and has simply followed the original shape of the block).

4   If necessary, features like nose and ears can be glued onto the head.

5   Beads and buttons are useful for eyes. Add hair and paint as required.

Note: (i) Appropriate tools for shaping foam rubber are *sharp* scissors (large dressmaker's scissors with plastic handles are especially useful), an old bread knife, a hacksaw blade (this can be held and used without hurting the hands) and a sharp knife. When using scissors, cut with small snips, not large cuts; when using a knife, *never* cut towards the hand holding the block.

(ii) When painting foam rubber, paint applied with a brush will soak into the foam and remain wet for a long time. To avoid this, mix the paint fairly thick and apply it to the surface of the foam with the fingers, rubbing it on.

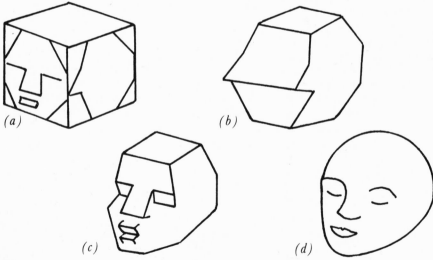

(a)   (b)   (c)   (d)

Figure 9

Polystyrene head

Materials: block of polystyrene (styrofoam), paper, paste

1 Draw, cut and shape the head in the same way as for a foam rubber head, described in the previous example. Tools to use are a bread knife, sharp craft knife, hacksaw blade and a selection of surform rasps (especially a small hand rasp). A battery-powered heated wire cutter is useful but is banned by many local education authorities because of the fumes given off; one can manage very well without one, however.
2 When the head is shaped (boldly), it should be covered with two or three layers of paper pasted on to strengthen it and prevent chipping. Use a decorating paste recommended for wallpaper and polystyrene tiles.
3 Paint and finish the head as required.

Figure 10 **Polystyrene heads at different stages of construction**

Features for instant puppets

The ideas for features illustrated (*Figure 11*) are simply suggestions. Many further ideas will present themselves and it pays always to keep an eye open for things to stock up and replenish a collection.

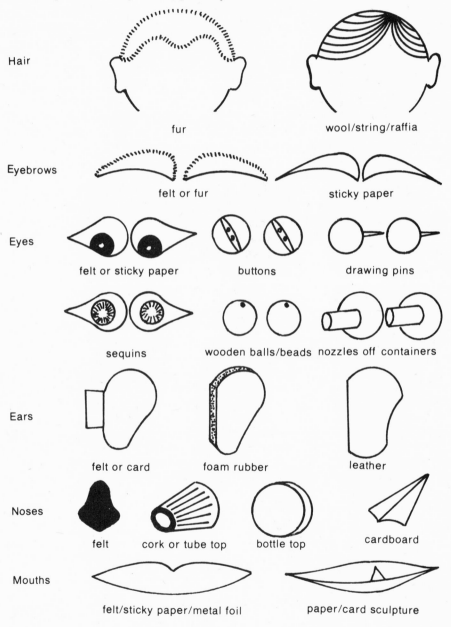

Hair

fur   wool/string/raffia

Eyebrows

felt or fur   sticky paper

Eyes

felt or sticky paper   buttons   drawing pins

sequins   wooden balls/beads   nozzles off containers

Ears

felt or card   foam rubber   leather

Noses

felt   cork or tube top   bottle top   cardboard

Mouths

felt/sticky paper/metal foil   paper/card sculpture

Figure 11

A puppet with 'instant' features

Glove puppet construction

Ball head puppet

Materials: an old ball, a large piece of material

1 In the ball, cut a hole just large enough for the index finger.
2 Add hair and features to the face.
3 Cut three small holes in the centre of the material (*Figure 12a*).
4 Put the material over the operator's hand so that the thumb and first two fingers protrude through the holes (*Figure 12b*).
5 Put the ball head onto the index finger (the neck), making the thumb and other finger the puppet's arms.

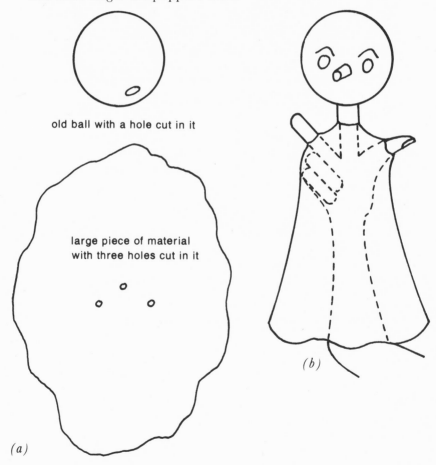

old ball with a hole cut in it

large piece of material
with three holes cut in it

(a)

(b)

Figure 12

Air-ball puppet

Materials: plastic air-ball, short dowel rod, large piece of material or scarf

1   Push the dowelling into the ball to form a nose.
2   Put the scarf over the hand (in the operating position).
3   Push the ball onto the index finger and put elastic bands around the thumb and second finger to make the puppet's arms.
4   This method avoids spoiling a large piece of material and enables costumes and features to be changed as required.

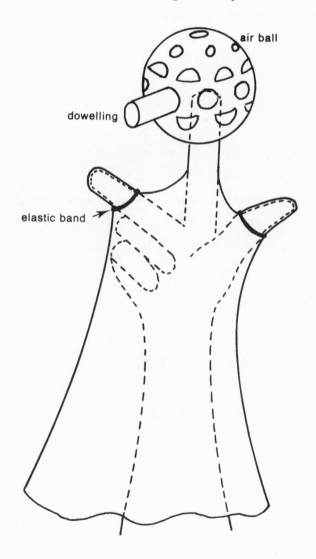

Figure 13

Making the glove

Materials: paper, fabric (curtain lining or jersey material are recommended), galvanized (coat-hanger) wire

1   Fold the sheet of paper in half (longways).
2   Lay one hand on the paper as illustrated (*Figure 14a*) in the operating position and draw round the outline, but not too close to the hand.
3   Make sure that: the neck of the glove is wide enough to go over the puppet's neck, the body is wide enough to get the hand in and out quickly, the pattern is long enough to reach the operator's elbow.
4   Cut out and lay the pattern on a double piece of material (inside out) and draw round the outline. Stitch around the outline, leaving the neck and the bottom of the glove open.
5   Try the glove for comfort; if it does not fit both hands comfortably, unpick and restitch before cutting out the glove.
6   Cut out the glove within $\frac{1}{4}$in (5mm) of the stitching and snip into the corners between neck and arms, cutting right up to the stitching otherwise these will not lay flat when the glove is reversed (*Figure 14b*).
7   Reverse the glove so that the seams are inside.
8   Make a piece of wire into the shape illustrated (*Figure 14c*), a circle with a loop at the back.
9   Glue or stitch up the hem of the glove around the wire, leaving the loop standing up at the back (*Figure 14d*).
10   Glue the neck of the glove around the puppet's neck, further securing it with a strong draw-thread if required (*Figure 14f*).

Note: (i) The wire in the hem holds the glove open for easy access and the loop acts as a hook for hanging the puppet upside down in the booth ready for immediate use (*Figure 14e*).

(ii) The method of operation shown here, with two fingers in the neck, is the recommended one. It will be found the most comfortable method of operation for most people and it allows more definite control of the head. Turning the head is also better effected by this method: press the two fingers apart against the inside of the neck moving them backwards and forwards to make the head rotate. Manipulation with one finger in the neck requires the whole hand (and therefore the whole of the puppet's body) to turn if the head is to turn.

(iii) It is recommended that the glove is made from curtain lining or jersey material and the costume then added—glued or sewn over the glove. This makes the glove and costume longer wearing and it is easier to get a good fit this way, rather than trying to make the glove directly from the costume materials.

(iv) It is a good idea to keep a small selection of ready-made gloves in different sizes and matching templates for them. Children can try them on and use as their pattern the template of whichever is most comfortable.

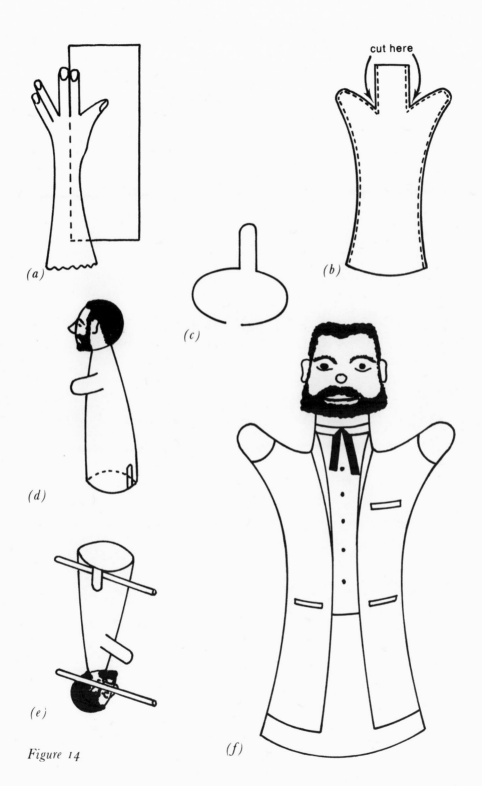

cut here

(a)

(b)

(c)

(d)

(e)

(f)

Figure 14

Felt puppet

Materials: sheet of paper, felt

1   First make a pattern for the glove as described in the previous example. Cut out the glove shape in the paper up to the neck (*Figure 15a*). Open out the paper, then add and cut out the head.
2   Use the pattern to cut out two felt shapes.
3   Put the shapes together and oversew all round the edge, leaving the bottom open (*Figure 15b*).
4   Add features and any pieces of costume required.

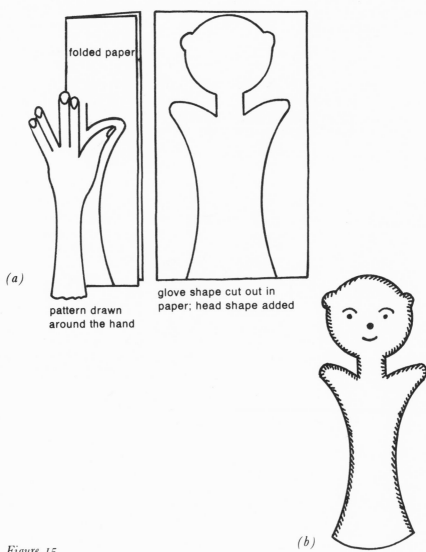

(a)

folded paper

pattern drawn
around the hand

glove shape cut out in
paper; head shape added

(b)

Figure 15

Carton head

Materials: plastic carton, cardboard, newspaper or foam rubber

1 Roll a strip of cardboard into a tube that will fit over two fingers. The tube should be at least $1-1\frac{1}{2}$ in $(3-4\,\text{cm})$ deeper than the carton. Secure the tube shape with strong glue or sellotape (*Figure 16a*).
2 Stuff one end of the tube with a little crumpled newspaper or foam rubber smeared with glue.
3 Glue this end of the tube and stand it in the carton.
4 Crumple small sheets of newspaper, glue them and stuff them in the head around the tube. Alternatively, secure the tube with glue and foam rubber (*Figure 16b*).
5 Glue a piece of thin white card or paper around the carton (*Figure 16c*).
6 Paint and add hair, features and a glove made by the standard method (*Figure 16d*).

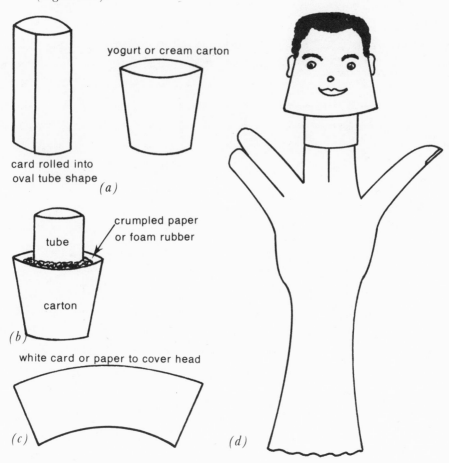

yogurt or cream carton

card rolled into oval tube shape
(a)

crumpled paper or foam rubber

tube

carton

(b)

white card or paper to cover head

(c) *(d)*

Figure 16

Cheesebox head

Materials: cheesebox, matchbox, cardboard, trimmings

1   Make two cuts in the sides of the lid and bottom of the cheesebox so that the matchbox will just fit between the cuts (*Figure 17a*).
2   Glue the matchbox into the bottom piece so that half is inside the box and half sticking out to make the neck (*Figure 17b*).
3   Glue the other side of the matchbox and the inside edge of the cheesebox lid.
4   Put the two parts of the cheesebox back together.
5   Glue a strip of thin cardboard around the edge of the box (*Figure 17c*).
6   Paint and add features, hair and the glove (*Figure 17d*).

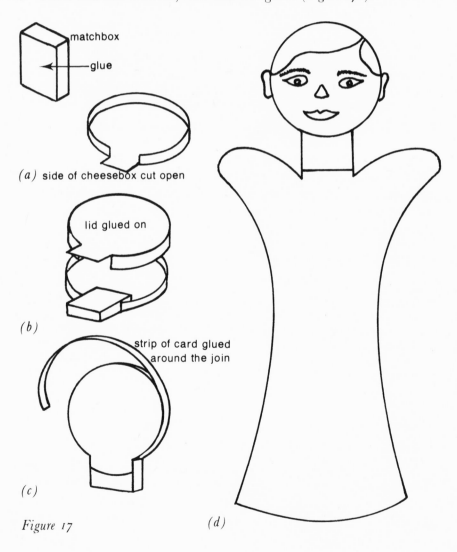

matchbox

glue

(*a*) side of cheesebox cut open

lid glued on

(*b*)

strip of card glued around the join

(*c*)

Figure 17   (*d*)

Animal head

Materials: plastic carton, cardboard, trimmings, newspaper

1   Roll a piece of card into a tube for the neck (it should take two fingers); glue or tape it securely.
2   Make a hole for the neck near the bottom of the carton (*Figure 18a*).
3   Glue inside one end of the tube and stuff the end with crumpled newspaper or foam rubber.
4   Glue this end of the tube and around the hole in the carton and push the neck securely in place.
5   Glue the inside of the carton (and the tube inside it) and stuff with crumpled newspaper or foam rubber to help secure the tube (*Figure 18b*).
6   Glue a piece of card over the end of the carton (*Figure 18b*). Glue thin white card or paper around the carton.
7   Paint and add trimmings for features and the glove (*Figure 18c*).

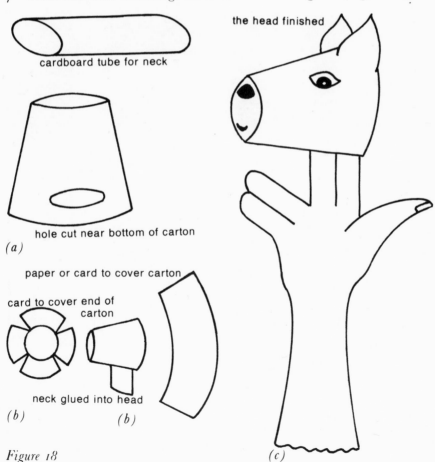

cardboard tube for neck

the head finished

hole cut near bottom of carton

(a)

paper or card to cover carton

card to cover end of carton

neck glued into head

(b)   *(b)*

Figure 18   *(c)*

57

Glove puppet with legs

Materials: as for a standard glove puppet (see pages 52–53), plus foam rubber and fabric

1   Make the puppet's head and glove by the standard methods, making sure the glove is long and made from a neutral coloured material (black, beige, etc.).
2   Cut legs and feet from foam rubber and glue the feet to the legs.
3   Make trouser legs and, if necessary, cover the feet (felt is useful for this).
4   Glue the tops of the legs securely to the glove at an appropriate point for the waist (*Figure 19a*).
5   Cover the tops of the legs with the puppet's jacket, etc. (*Figure 19b*).

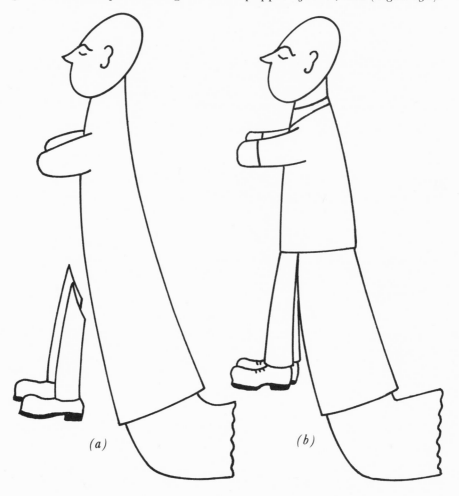

(a)   *(b)*

Figure 19

Sock puppet

Materials: an old sock, trimmings

1   Insert the hand into a sock cut off halfway down the foot (smear the cut edge with glue to prevent fraying).
2   Hold the hand in the operating position (fingers together on top and thumb underneath).
3   Tuck what is left of the foot back inside the sock between the thumb and fingers to form the mouth (*Figure 20a*).
4   Add features and trimmings as required (*Figure 20b*).

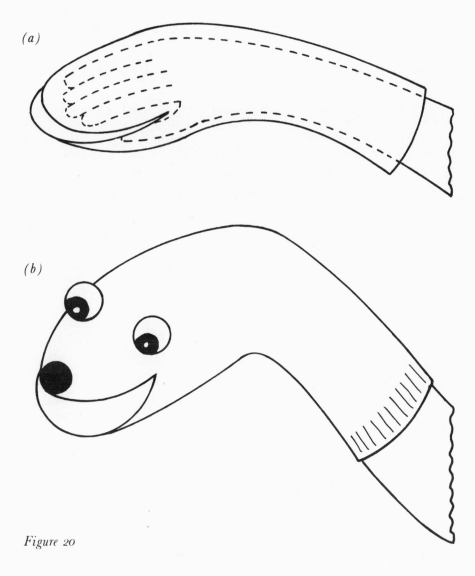

(a)

(b)

Figure 20

Sleeve puppet

Materials: cardboard picnic plate, cardboard, fabric, foam rubber, trimmings

1   Fold the centre of the picnic plate into the shape illustrated (*Figure 21a*). Glue fabric along the fold to reinforce it.
2   Bend two strips of card into the shape illustrated (*Figure 21b*) and glue one on the top and one on the bottom of the folded plate to hold the fingers and thumb for manipulation.
3   Pad the top and bottom of the plate to the required shape with foam rubber, glued on (*Figure 21c*).
4   Take a piece of fabric just over twice as wide as the plate and a little longer than from finger tips to elbow. Stitch the long edges together with the material inside out (*Figure 21d*) then reverse this 'sleeve' so that the seam is inside.
5   Put the plate in the end of the sleeve and make two cuts along the material for the sides of the mouth (*Figure 21e*).
6   Glue the material to the edges of the plate (*Figure 21f*) and add features and trimmings (*Figure 21g*), including a lining for the mouth to cover the edges of the sleeve.
7   Slip an arm into the sleeve to hold the plate and move the mouth.

Eggbox head

Materials: as for a sleeve puppet, described previously, but with an eggbox instead of a picnic plate

1   Reinforce the hinge of the eggbox by gluing a piece of strong fabric along it.
2   Cut off the flap that normally secures the lid closed.
3   Follow the same principles as for making the sleeve puppet (see previous example). The eggbox may be used either widthways or longways as the basis for the head.

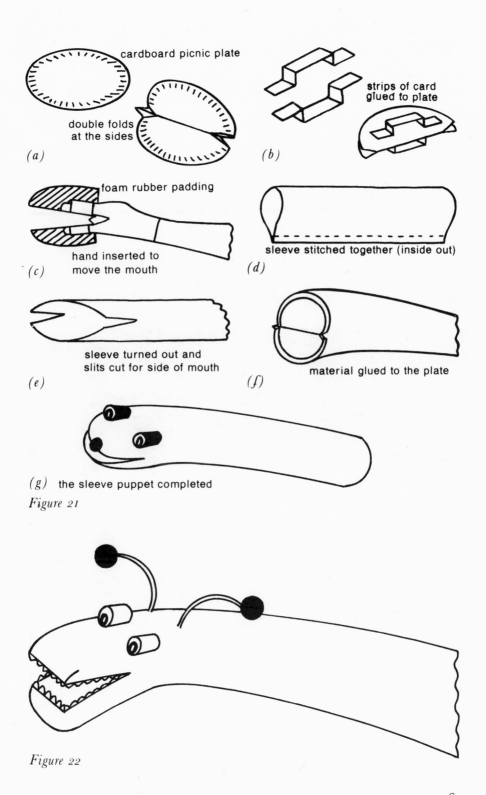

(a) cardboard picnic plate
double folds at the sides

(b) strips of card glued to plate

(c) foam rubber padding
hand inserted to move the mouth

(d) sleeve stitched together (inside out)

(e) sleeve turned out and slits cut for side of mouth

(f) material glued to the plate

(g) the sleeve puppet completed

Figure 21

Figure 22

Rod puppet construction

Paper plate rod puppet

Materials: picnic plate, an old stick or rod, sticky tape, fabric and trimmings

1 Attach the rod to the back of the plate by means of tape (*Figure 23a*).
2 Wrap a little tape around the stick at the base of the neck.
3 Tie fabric for the costume securely to the rod just above the tape (the tape prevents the costume sliding down the rod).
4 Paint the face, add features, hair, etc. as required (*Figure 23b*).

Note: This puppet may also be used as a rod-and-hand puppet (see page 74).

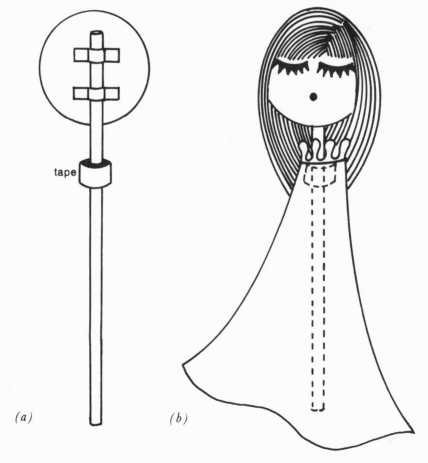

tape

(a)   (b)

Figure 23

Dish mop rod puppet

Materials: dish mop, plastic air ball, clothes peg, fabric and trimmings if required

1   Push the handle of the mop through the holes in the ball and push the ball right up to the mop.
2   Clip the clothes peg into two of the holes in the ball to make a nose. The puppet is ready to use as it is (*Figure 24b*). This sort of rod puppet without a body is called a *marot* (or *marotte*).
3   Alternatively, a costume may be added, draped around the rod and secured at the neck by an elastic band (*Figure 24c*).

(a)   *(b)*   *(c)*

Figure 24

Free-standing carton puppet

Materials: yogurt or cream carton, washing-up liquid container, drawing pin, short piece of dowelling, cardboard, fabric and trimmings

1 The head is a yogurt or cream carton; press the drawing pin through the bottom of the carton into the end of a wooden dowel (*Figure 25b*).
2 Pull the nozzle off the top of a washing-up liquid container (the body) and glue the dowel into the neck of the container (*Figure 25c*). If necessary, to ensure a tight fit, glue paper or card around the dowel first.
3 Glue a piece of fabric over the body; cut sleeves from the same fabric and glue them to the sides of the body.
4 Make hands from felt or cardboard and glue them into the sleeves (*Figure 25d*).
5 Glue a piece of card over the top of the head and another piece of card or paper around the head; then paint and add features and hair.

This puppet may be held and moved from the bottom of the bottle and may be stood in a display when not in use.

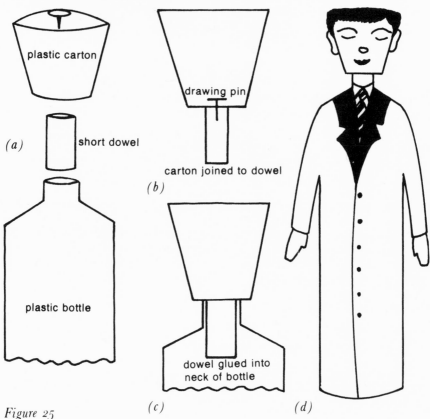

plastic carton

(a) short dowel

plastic bottle

drawing pin

carton joined to dowel

(b)

dowel glued into
neck of bottle

Figure 25

(c) *(d)*

Carton rod puppet

Materials: cartons or containers of various shapes and sizes, dowel rod, masking tape, nail or drawing pin, fabric and trimmings

1 Secure an empty container for the head to the top of the dowel rod; glue it to the top of the rod and further secure with a nail or drawing pin pushed through the carton (*Figure 26a*). To secure some cartons, it is a good idea also to smear the top of the rod and the carton with glue and push in a little foam rubber (*Figure 26b*).
2 Glue and tape another carton to the rod for shoulders.
3 Make the arms from toilet roll or Smarties tubes, strung together and suspended by string from the shoulder carton (*Figure 26a*).
4 Hands cut from card are tied to the arms.
5 Alternatively, hands may be cut from foam rubber; if so, a little foam should be left at the wrist to glue into the end of the arm tube (*Figure 26c*).
6 Dress and finish the puppet as desired.

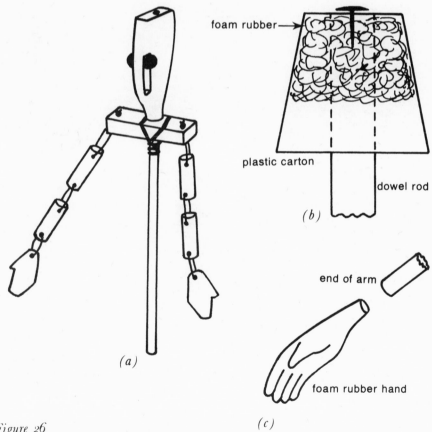

foam rubber→

plastic carton

dowel rod

(b)

end of arm

foam rubber hand

(a)

(c)

Figure 26

Rod puppet with turning head

Materials: plastic carton, $\frac{1}{2}$ in (12 mm) diameter dowelling, cardboard, foam rubber, fabric and trimmings

1   Make and secure the head on the rod as described in the previous example.
2   For the shoulders, cut a cardboard disc a little larger than the head carton. This may be padded with foam rubber if required (*Figure 27b*).
3   Make holes near the edge of the disc for attaching arms.
4   Cut a hole in the middle of the disc and push the rod through the hole.
5   Hold the disc in place and glue a strip of cardboard around the rod under the disc so that the shoulders cannot slip down the rod (*Figure 27b*).
6   Add arms and costume and finish the head as desired (*Figure 27c*).

Alternatively, at stage 2, use a cardboard box or other suitable container instead of the disc to form the shoulders.

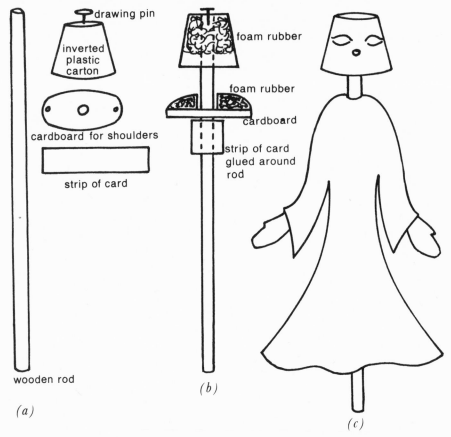

Figure 27

An alternative turning head

Materials: as for previous turning head, plus a long cardboard tube

1   Fix the head on the end of a rod, as before (*Figure 28a*).
2   Fix the shoulders to the cardboard tube with the top of the tube projecting above the shoulders for the neck (*Figure 28b*).
3   Add arms and hands.
4   Put the head rod inside the cardboard tube.
5   Hold the puppet by holding the tube; move the head by turning the rod with the other hand (*Figure 28c*).
6   With this method it is also possible to raise and lower the head.
7   To effect one-handed operation, cut a small slot in the cardboard tube (*Figure 29a*).
8   Drill a small hole in the wooden rod and glue into the hole, through the slot, the end of a piece of coat-hanger wire bent into a thumb rest, as illustrated.
9   Hold the tube with one hand and effect head movements with the thumb on the wire (*Figure 29b*). This leaves the other hand free to operate the hand rods.

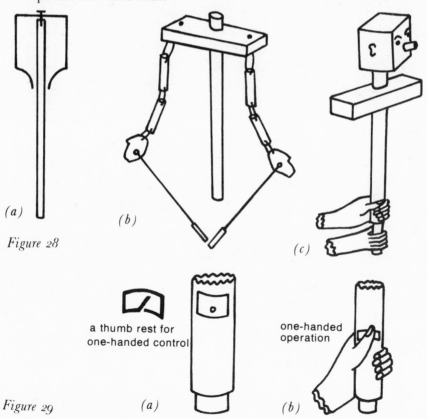

(a)

Figure 28

(b)

(c)

a thumb rest for one-handed control

one-handed operation

Figure 29   *(a)*   *(b)*

Rod puppet with flexible waist

Materials: as for previous rod puppets

1   A puppet with a long rod cannot bend at the waist. It bends, with a stiff back, from the ankles (*Figure 30a*).
2   In order to effect waist movements, use a shorter rod and hold it with the hand up inside the costume. The performer's wrist then becomes the puppet's waist and makes possible a wider range of movements (*Figure 30b*).

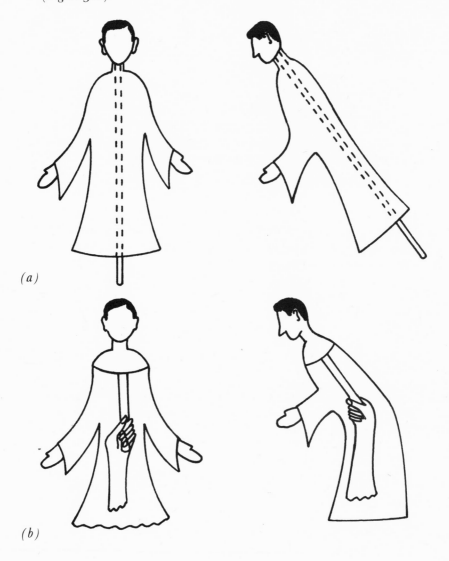

(a)

(b)

Figure 30

Balloon head

Materials: balloon, cardboard tube, cartons, trimmings and fabric, dowel rod (optional)

1 Blow up the balloon and knot it securely.
2 Tie a thread to the balloon. Thread the end through a small hole made in the cardboard tube and knot the thread to secure the balloon head on the tube (*Figure 31a*). Alternatively, secure the balloon with masking tape to the tube or a rod.
3 Add features and hair to the balloon (*Figure 31b*)—self-adhesive labels (coloured spots, etc.) are especially useful for features. Double-sided tape is good for fixing hair to the balloon: stick the tape to the balloon, then press the hair (wool, raffia, etc.) onto the other side of the tape.
4 Make the rest of the puppet by any method described in this section.

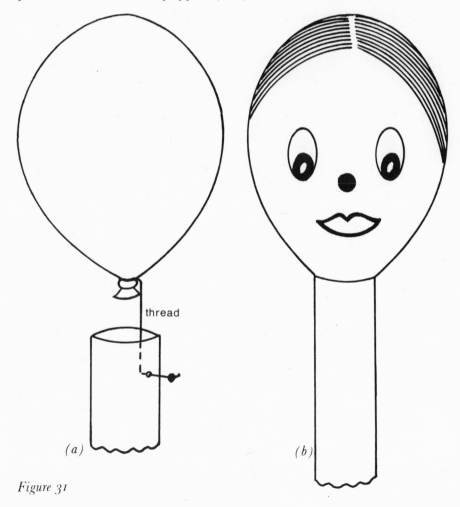

Figure 31

Cardboard head

Materials: corrugated card or plain card, cardboard tube or dowel rod, trimmings

1 Roll a piece of corrugated or plain card into a tubular or conical shape for the head. Glue and tape it in the required shape.
2 Glue on features sculpted in card (*Figure 32a*).
3 Add hair (raffia, wool, strips of paper or card, etc.).
4 Fix the head to the rod or cardboard tube with tape or glue and card, pushing drawing pins through the back of the head into the rod (*Figure 32b*).
5 Add body, arms, etc. as required.

(a)   (b)

Figure 32

Nodding head

Materials: large carton or cardboard head, galvanized (coat-hanger) wire, cardboard, thread

1   Drill a small hole across the top of the rod.
2   Make a hole in each side of the carton that is to be the head.
3   Push a piece of coat-hanger wire through one side of the head, through the top of the rod and out the other side of the head, so that the carton pivots on the rod (*Figure 33a*).
4   Bend over the ends of the wire.
5   Make 'spacers' on each side of the rod (to stop the rod moving from the centre of the head) from card glued or taped into tube shapes around the wire. Alternatively, make the spacers from pieces of foam rubber glued onto each side of the wire.
6   If a head control is required (as opposed to a head which is balanced and allowed to move naturally as the puppet moves), make sure the head pivots so that it falls forwards, i.e. place the wire further back in the head.
7   Fix a thread to the back of the carton (make a hole and tie it on). Tie the other end of the thread to a lever on the rod (*Figure 33b*). The lever is made from a piece of wire, bent to shape, with the ends pushed into a hole drilled across the rod.
8   Press the lever with the thumb to raise the head. Release the lever and the weight of the head brings it down.

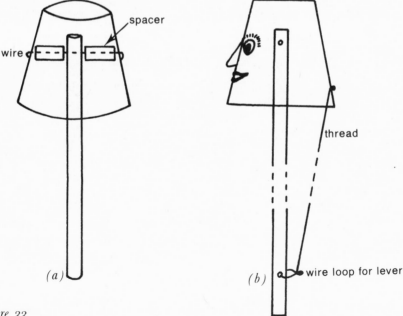

Figure 33

Rod puppet with hand controls

Materials: as for any rod puppet, plus dowelling, thread and galvanized (coat-hanger) wire

1   The basic puppet is made and dressed in one of the ways described previously.
2   The hand controls are made from coat-hanger wire. With a pair of pliers, make a small loop in one end of the wire and seal the closure of the loop with glue.
3   Tie one end of a piece of thread to the loop and thread the other end through a hole in the hand; tie it securely to a small button (*Figure 34b*).
4   Make a loop in the other end of the wire for holding it or, preferably, drill a small hole in a short dowel and push and glue the wire into the rod (*Figure 34a*).

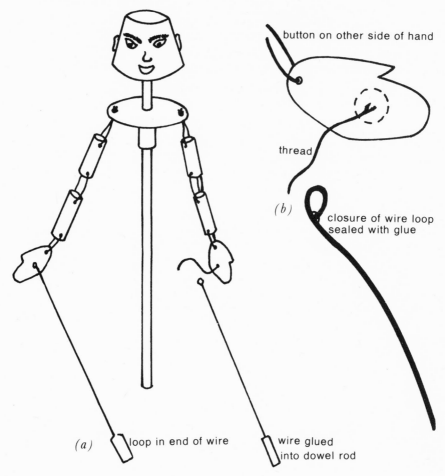

Figure 34

Manipulating hand controls

1   Hold the main rod in either hand, using this to effect movements of the head and the body.
2   With the other hand pick up one of the hand wires and move the puppet's hand and arm (*Figure 35a*).
3   With practice one hand can hold and move both wires at the same time (for this the dowel handles are a great advantage) (*Figure 35b*).
4   Instead of letting one arm hang loose, the operator can hold its wire with a little finger of the hand holding the main rod (*Figure 35c*).

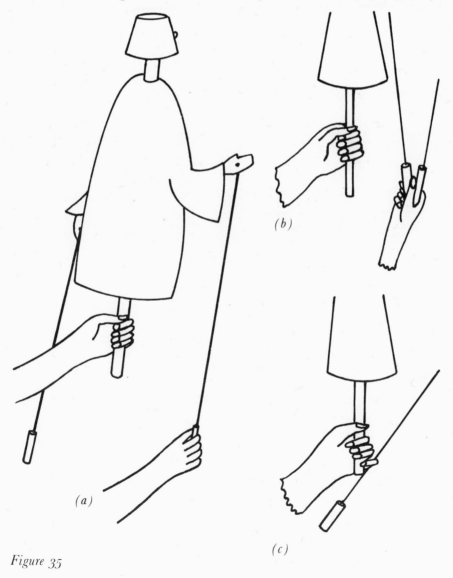

(b)

(a)

(c)

Figure 35

Rod-and-hand puppet

Materials: as for previous rod puppets

1   This puppet is held by a rod like other rod puppets, but the operator's hand is used as one of the puppet's hands. Make the basic puppet as for any other figure and dress it with a fairly full robe.
2   Decide where on the robe the hand looks best and make a slit here.
3   Stitch around the cut edges to stop them fraying. A little elastic may be stitched around the slit if desired, to ensure a snug fit around the wrist.
4   To operate the puppet, hold the rod with one hand and push the other hand through the slit. It is usual to wear a glove on this hand as it is more in keeping with the puppet than the human hand (*Figure 36a*).
5   A slit may be made in each side of the robe so that a different hand can be used, or a second operator may provide both hands of the puppet.
6   An alternative arrangement is to have a proper costume with sleeves instead of the robe (*Figure 36b*); the operator's hand fits into one sleeve below the elbow and provides the hand; the other sleeve is stuffed and a foam rubber hand of appropriate size is glued into the cuff.

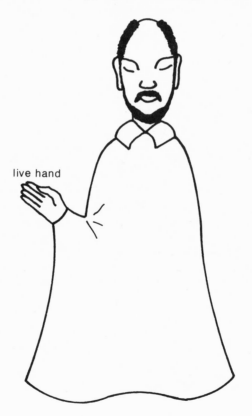

live hand

Figure 36 (a)

Figure 36(b) A rod-and-hand puppet

Animal rod puppet

Materials: plastic cartons, foam rubber, cardboard, drawing pins, two
$\frac{1}{2}$in (12mm) diameter dowel rods, fabric and trimmings

1 Cut two holes near the front rim of the body carton, one on top, just
   large enough for a rod to pass through, and one immediately below it
   but a little larger.
2 Glue a long strip of cardboard and wrap it around the rod so that the
   top of the body can rest on the card as illustrated.
3 Make a cardboard washer, place it on the rod on top of the card, then
   insert the rod into the body.
4 Place another cardboard washer on top of the body; then glue another
   wider strip of card around the rod above the body. This forms the neck
   and prevents the rod dropping down in the body.
5 Make a small hole near the bottom of the head carton and glue the rod
   into it.
6 Secure the rod with a drawing pin through the carton into the end of
   the rod and with a little foam rubber glued and pushed into the bottom
   of the carton around the rod.
7 Make a hole for the second rod near the back of the body; secure it with
   a drawing pin or a nail through the top of the carton.
8 Add foam rubber legs and feet (glued to the body) and cover the body
   with fur fabric or any other suitable material. Finish with features and
   trimmings.

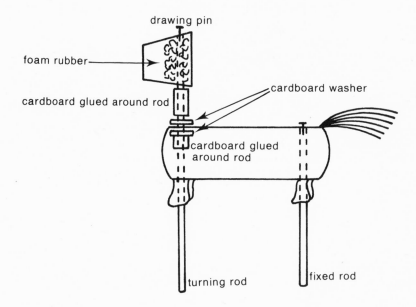

Figure 37

Another animal rod puppet

Materials: sheet of thin foam rubber, block of foam rubber or a carton, coathanger wire, dowelling, cord

1. Make the head from foam rubber or a carton as described in earlier examples (see pages 46 and 55).
2. Securely glue one end of a fairly thick piece of cord into the head; the cord is the basis for the body.
3. Thread and glue onto the cord discs of foam rubber separated by smaller foam washers.
4. Attach two control wires—one to the head and another near the tail.

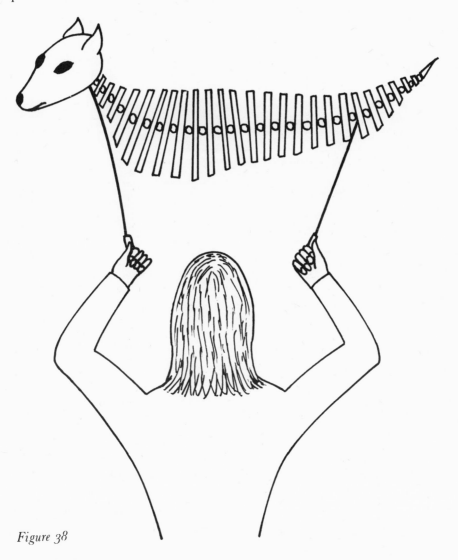

Figure 38

Advanced rod puppet construction

1   Methods for making heads are described on pages 40–49. They may be made with or without the nodding or turning movements described earlier.

2   Shoulders cut in foam are based on a plywood or hardboard shape, supported by card glued around the rod (*Figure 39b*).

3   The arms are made from foam rubber or balsa wood (with a fabric or leather joint) or from dowelling (with a leather or screw-eye joint).

4   The hands are made from foam rubber or wood.

5   If the puppet needs to have legs visible to the audience, first cut a hardboard or plywood shape (like the shoulder-piece) to serve as the hips.

6   Make the legs and feet from foam rubber or balsa, with fabric or leather joints.

7   Secure the legs to the hips by strong cords through the tops of the legs; the ends pass through holes in the hip plate and the ends of the cords are knotted *(Figure 39a)*.

8   Glue one end of a tube of fabric onto the shoulders and the other end to the hips.

9   Dress and finish the puppet as desired.

Note: Details for making and jointing the limbs are described in the Marionette section (see pages 88–93).

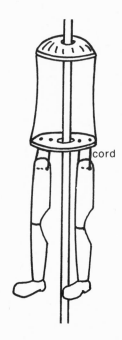

(a)

Figure 39

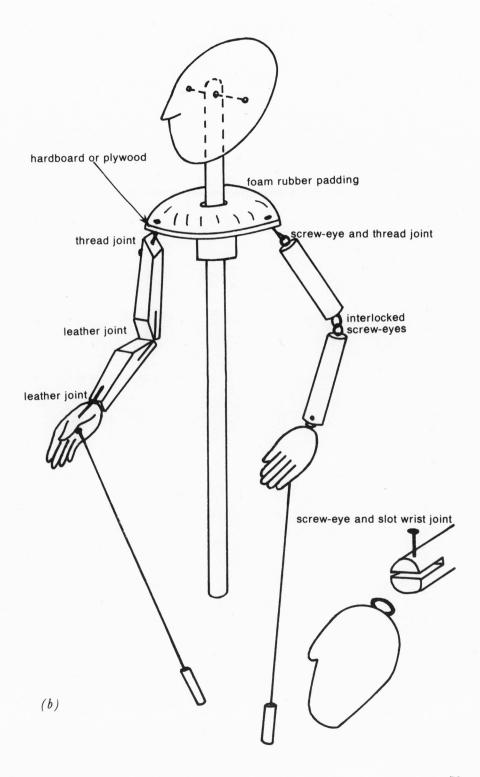

hardboard or plywood

foam rubber padding

thread joint

screw-eye and thread joint

leather joint

interlocked
screw-eyes

leather joint

screw-eye and slot wrist joint

(b)

Marionette construction

Scarf marionette

Materials: old ball, large piece of material, dowel rod, thread, felt

1   Put the ball in the centre of the material.
2   Gather up the material around the ball and tie a piece of thread around it for the puppet's neck.
3   Thread a long piece of thin string through a large darning needle and push the needle through the ball.
4   Tie both ends of the string to the dowel rod; the strings should be long enough for the puppet to stand on the floor when the rod is held just above waist height.
5   Pick up a piece of material for the hand and tie a string around it; tie the other end of the string to the dowel. Do the same for the other hand.
6   Cut out pieces of felt for features and add any other trimmings desired.

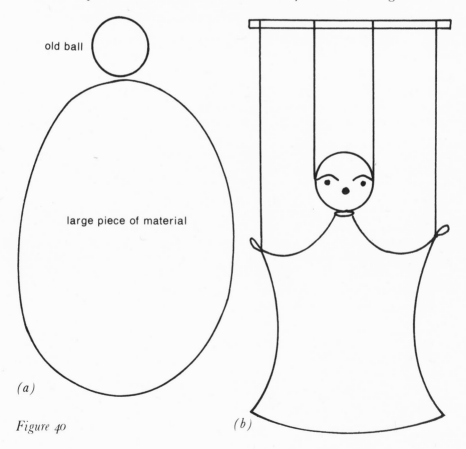

Figure 40

Carton marionette

Cartons can be joined together in many ways to create a marionette. *Figure 41* is just an example. A variety of methods for making marionette parts and joints with cartons and other materials are given in the following pages.

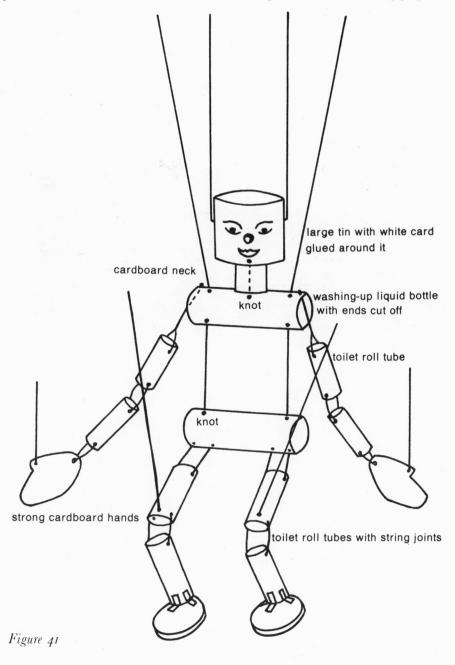

large tin with white card
glued around it

cardboard neck

knot

washing-up liquid bottle
with ends cut off

toilet roll tube

knot

strong cardboard hands

toilet roll tubes with string joints

Figure 41

Animal marionette

The same principles apply to the construction of animal marionettes as to the carton marionette described previously. *Figure 42* shows one example of cartons used for four-legged animals.

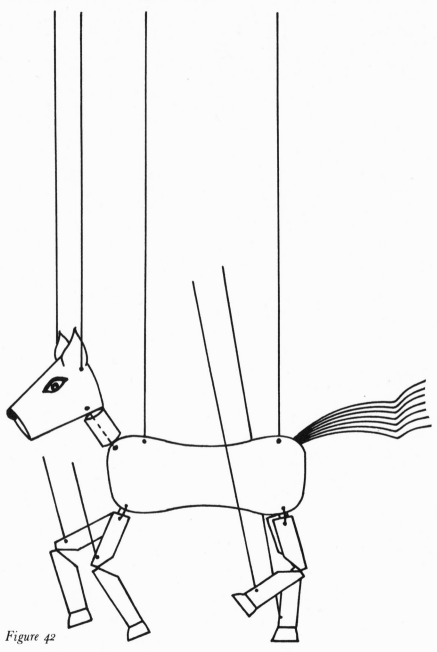

Figure 42

Snake marionette

Materials: balsa wood, cotton reels, cord, fabric and trimmings

1 Make the head from balsa wood, shaped with a file or rasp. A saw cut will form the mouth.
2 Drill a hole through the head, from the back through to the mouth.
3 Knot the end of a piece of cord (and seal the knot with glue) and thread the other end through the mouth. Pull the cord right through until the knot is inside the mouth.
4 Thread cotton reels onto the cord to make the body (a bead between each cotton reel will help to make the body more flexible). Knot the cord at the tail.
5 The shape of the end of the tail can be added using balsa wood or foam rubber glued on.
6 Cover the body with a tube of fabric.
7 Add control strings as required (head, neck and tail are recommended). Secure head and neck strings to the front of a wooden bar; thread the tail string through a hole drilled in the rear of the bar and tie it to a curtain ring—pull the ring to raise the tail.

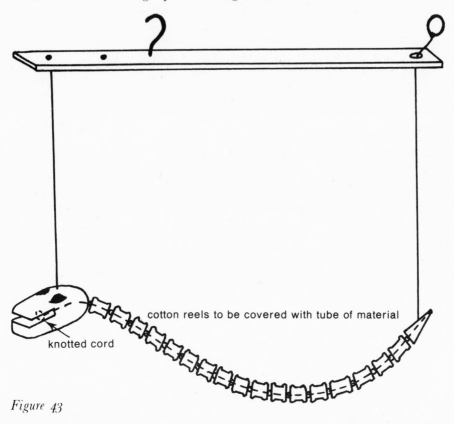

cotton reels to be covered with tube of material

knotted cord

Figure 43

Useful methods for making marionette parts and joints

Heads and necks

Heads may be made from cartons or by any of the techniques described at the beginning of Part Two. *Figures 44–46* show various means of jointing heads made by different techniques.

1 A carton head may be joined to the body with knotted string, using a cardboard tube or cotton reel for the neck (*Figure 44a*).

2 An inverted carton head may have a more advanced top neck joint: the neck is dowelling with a screw-eye in each end; the carton pivots on the neck by means of a piece of wire pushed through the sides of the head and through the screw-eye (*Figure 44b*). Cardboard tubes or foam rubber are placed on the wire on each side of the neck to stop sideways movement. Loop the ends of the wire for securing head strings.

3 A similar technique is possible with foam rubber, polystyrene and modelled heads (*Figure 44c*). The neck, made from dowelling, fits into a slot in the head and is secured with wire as before. Spacers will be necessary on each side of the neck with a hollow modelled head but not with the solid foam rubber or polystyrene heads. The joint for foam and polystyrene heads may be strengthened by gluing into the head the top of a slim plastic container, as illustrated.

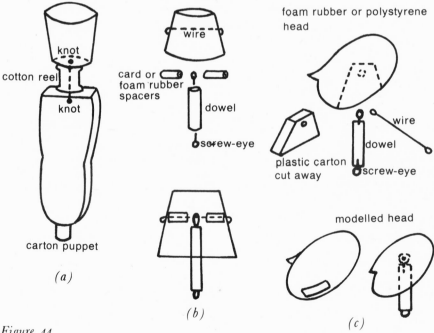

Figure 44

4   For a head and neck in one piece, a secure fixture will still be needed for the neck joint and head strings: glue a dowel into the head and fix a screw-eye in the bottom of the dowel (*Figure 45a*). If the ears are appropriately placed and made from a strong material, the tops of the ears may be used for securing head strings (*Figure 45b*). With more fragile materials or unsuitable ears, drill a hole across the upright dowel before inserting it in the head; after inserting the dowel, push a strong wire through the head and the hole in the dowel (*Figure 45c*). Loop the ends for attaching head strings.

5   A joint permitting very good turning and nodding action is shown in *Figure 46*. A cord is threaded through a hole in the mid-point of a dowel and knotted on top. Then the dowel is glued in the head. Screw-eyes through the head into the ends of the dowel help to secure it and provide fixtures for head strings. The cord is threaded through the neck (cardboard tube/cotton reel/dowel with hole drilled through the centre) and tied to the body.

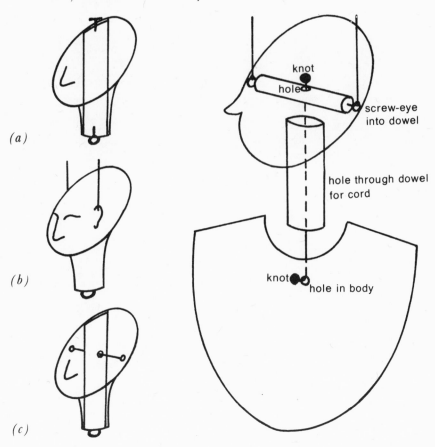

(a)

(b)

(c)

knot

hole

screw-eye
into dowel

hole through dowel
for cord

knot

hole in body

Figure 45   Figure 46

Neck/body joints

1 The neck of a carton puppet may be joined by a cord through the body carton, with the end knotted (*Figure 47a*). If there is any problem in tying the knot in the carton, tie and glue the cord to a short thin dowel (even a matchstick will do for a light puppet), then push the dowel through the hole, so that it secures the cord as illustrated (*Figure 47b*).
2 A dowelling neck may be joined to the body by a screw-eye (in the bottom of the dowel) and thread (through a hole in the body) (*Figure 47c*).
3 A dowelling neck may be joined to the body by a piece of strong wire through the body and a screw-eye in the dowel (*Figure 47d*).

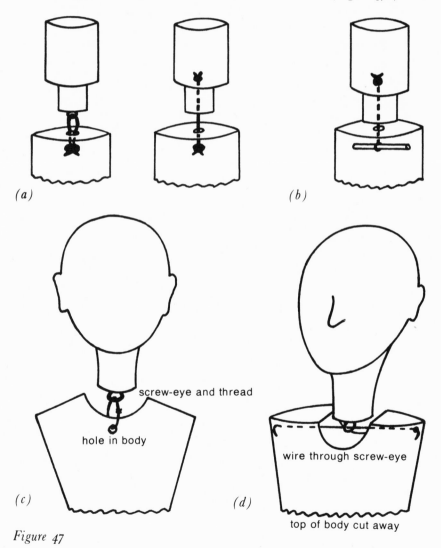

Figure 47

Bodies

1   Cartons can provide various interesting body shapes. These may have no waist joint or they may be joined by knotted cord to make a waist (*Figure 48a*).

2   Bodies may be made from strong card, hardboard or plywood, joined at the waist with cord and padded with foam rubber (*Figure 48b*). It is a good idea to thread the cord through a wooden bead as it provides smoother waist movement.

3   The padded body may also be joined by a strip of strong fabric, such as calico, or soft leather. The joining strip is glued to the two body pieces, leaving a space for the waist, then the padding is added (*Figure 48c*).

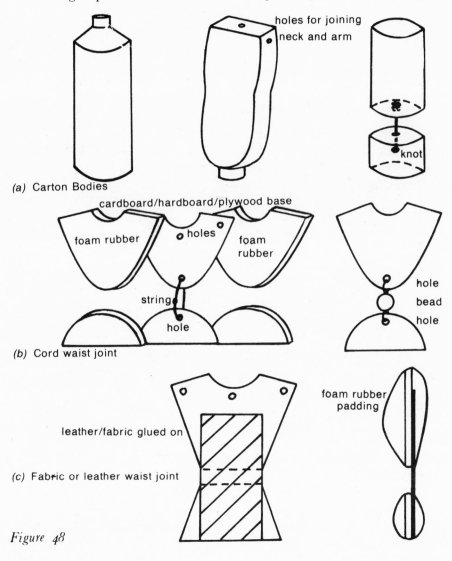

(a) Carton Bodies

(b) Cord waist joint

(c) Fabric or leather waist joint

Figure 48

Arms

1 The arms may be made from rope or cord, tied to the body (*Figure 49a*).
2 Strips of card may be glued around the cord to give some bulk (*Figure 49b*).
3 Foam rubber, trimmed to shape, may be threaded and glued on the cord (*Figure 49c*). To thread the cord through the foam, make a loop in the end of a piece of wire, thread it like a needle and push the wire through the foam.
4 A dowelling forearm, with screw-eye in the top, may be joined to the body by cord (*Figure 49d*).
5 Two dowels may be joined at the elbow by interlocked screw-eyes and at the shoulder by a screw-eye and thread (*Figure 49e*).
6 Cardboard tubes may be joined at the elbow by cutting away the card to permit bending and joining the parts with masking tape or fabric stuck on with glue (*Figure 49f*). The arms are joined to the shoulders by thread.
7 Dowelling or balsa wood arms may be joined similarly with a strap joint. First cut slots in each piece of the arm at the elbow, then cut or file away the wood on one side of the slot, to permit bending. Glue a piece of soft leather or strong fabric into the slots (*Figure 49g*); it must be short enough to allow the arm pieces to touch. Secure the strap with a nail or dressmaker's pins (in balsa). Join to the shoulders with cord through the body and the tops of the arms, knotted at the end.

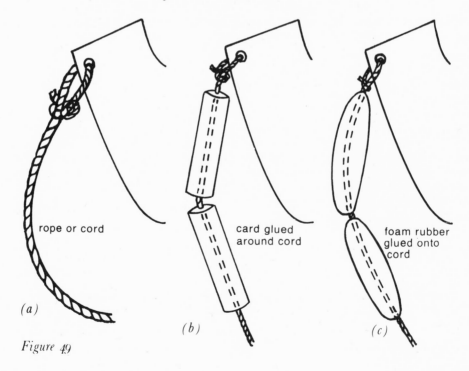

rope or cord

card glued around cord

foam rubber glued onto cord

(a)

(b)

(c)

Figure 49

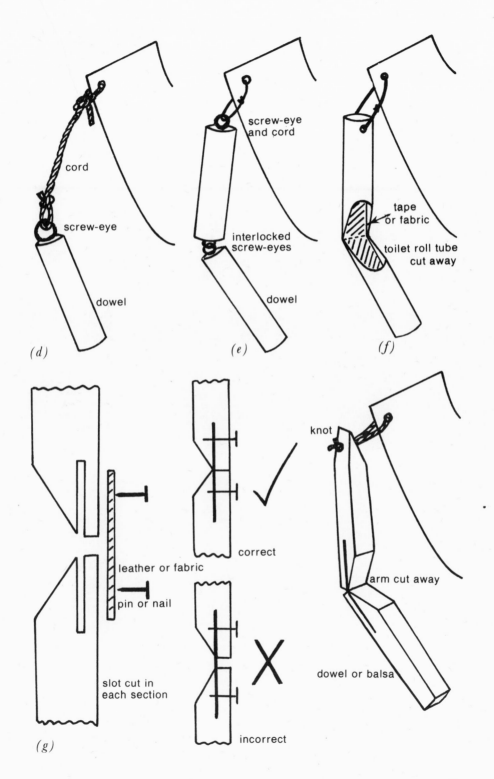

cord

screw-eye

dowel

(d)

screw-eye
and cord

interlocked
screw-eyes

dowel

(e)

tape
or fabric

toilet roll tube
cut away

(f)

leather or fabric

pin or nail

slot cut in
each section

(g)

correct

✓

incorrect

✗

knot

arm cut away

dowel or balsa

Hands

1 Hands may be cut from strong card or shaped from wood or foam rubber.

2 *Figure 50* shows the main shaping to make to avoid having flat, lifeless hands.

3 Cut foam rubber with sharp scissors.

4 Wood may be shaped easily with one or two surform rasps; these make the work so easy and safe that it is within the capabilities of a nine- or ten-year-old, but the wood must be held in a vice for effective working. It pays to leave a little extra waste at the wrist for securing in the vice and to cut off the waste when the rest of the hand is finished.

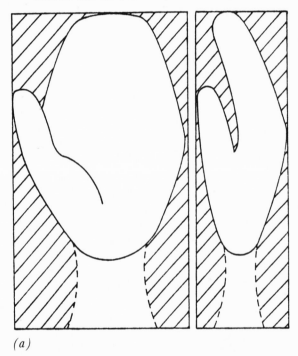

(a)

Figure 50   (b)

Wrist joints

1. Card hands may be joined to the arms with cord (*Figure 51a*).
2. Hands made from two pieces of card may be joined at the wrist by a strip of strong fabric or soft leather. One end is glued between the two layers of card; the other end is glued into a slot cut in the arm (*Figure 51b*).
3. A similar method may be used for foam rubber or wooden hands. A slot is cut in the hand, into which is glued fabric or leather. The other end of this strap is glued into a slot in the arm (*Figure 51b*).
4. The end of a cord arm may be glued into a hole cut in a foam rubber hand (*Figure 51c*).
5. A screw-eye may be fixed into the end of a wooden hand (*Figure 51d*) or into a dowel glued into a foam rubber hand (*Figure 51e*). The screw-eye may be used for the wrist joint by tying on a cord (*Figure 51f*), by interlocking a screw-eye in the arm (*Figure 51g*), or by pivoting the screw-eye in a slot in the arm, secured with a small nail (*Figure 51h*).

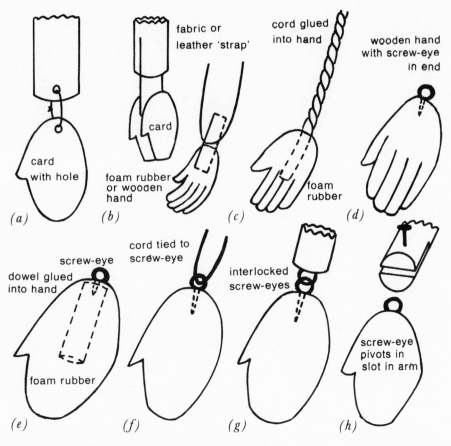

Figure 51

91

Legs and knee joints

1 Cardboard tube legs may be joined by cord for floppy joints or by tape or fabric, as for a carton elbow joint (*Figures 49f and 52a*).

2 Balsa wood or dowel legs (shaped by a rasp or file) may be joined with a fabric or leather 'strap joint', also described for elbows (*Figures 49g and 52b*).

3 A dowelling leg may also have a screw-eye knee joint (*Figure 52c*). Cut a slot in the end of one leg part; fix a screw-eye in the end of the other part. Cut or file away the legs as illustrated to permit bending. Insert the screw-eye in the slot and secure with a small nail.

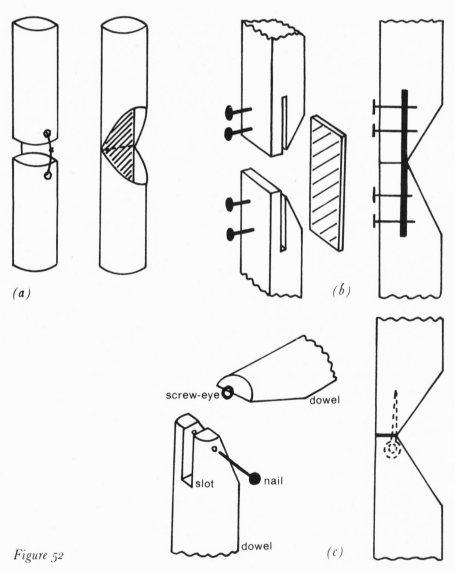

(a)

(b)

screw-eye

dowel

slot

nail

dowel

(c)

Figure 52

Feet and ankle joints

1 For a carton puppet, carton feet may be glued to the legs and further secured with tape or paste and paper (*Figure 53a*).

2 Balsa and foam rubber feet and legs may be glued together or the leg may be glued into a hole cut in the foot (*Figure 53b*). Joints in balsa may be reinforced with a long nail if required.

3 For wooden or balsa wood feet, balsa or dowelling legs may be tapered at the ends and held (by a nail) in slots cut in the feet (*Figure 53c*). Make the slot long enough to allow a little ankle movement, but not too much or the toe will drag as the puppet walks. The slot may be made by drilling a series of close holes and cleaned out with a craft knife or small file.

4 A screw-eye in the end of dowelling legs may be secured similarly in a slot in a wood or balsa wood foot (*Figure 53d*).

5 Wooden feet are shaped with the same tools as wooden hands.

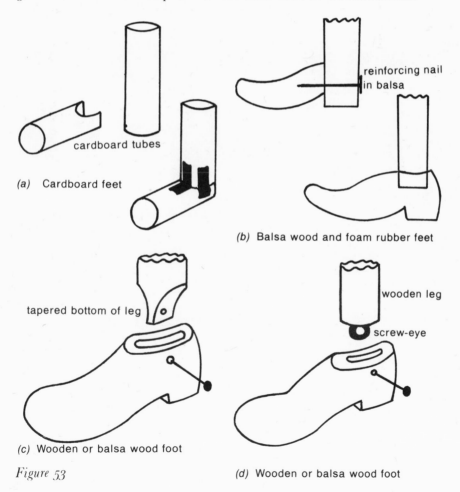

cardboard tubes

reinforcing nail in balsa

(a) Cardboard feet

(b) Balsa wood and foam rubber feet

tapered bottom of leg

wooden leg

screw-eye

(c) Wooden or balsa wood foot

Figure 53

(d) Wooden or balsa wood foot

Hip joints

1   Any type of leg may be attached to the body by cord through the tops of the legs; the cord is then threaded through holes in the pelvis and knotted (*Figure 54a*).

2   Alternatively, a similar method may be used with wire through the tops of the legs and attached to the body (*Figure 54b*).

3   For all except carton legs, a loop of leather or strong fabric over a piece of wire may form the joint. The wire is attached to the pelvis and the ends of the loop of leather are glued and pinned (or nailed, as appropriate) into a slot cut in the top of the leg (*Figure 54c*).

4   Similarly, one end of a piece of leather or fabric may be secured in a slot in the leg and glued to the hip (*Figure 54d*). If the waist is joined by a strip of fabric or leather (see *Figure 48c*), a longer joining piece can be used so that it also serves for attaching the legs.

5   Dowelling legs may also be joined by wire, with the legs suspended by screw-eyes fixed into the ends of the dowels (*Figure 54e*). Small pieces of dowelling with holes drilled through the centre may be threaded on the wire as spacers to stop sideways movement of the screw-eyes.

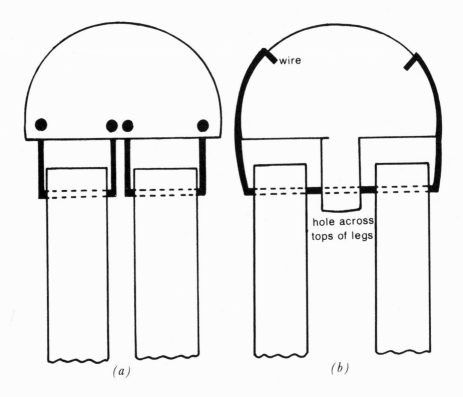

Figure 54

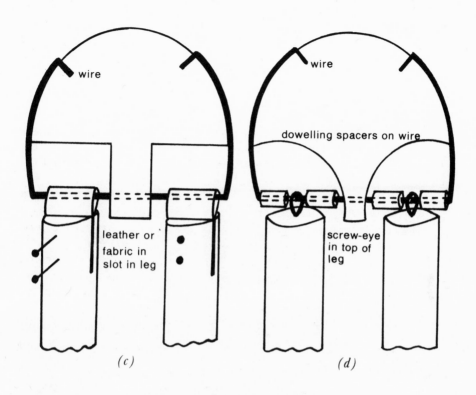

wire

wire

dowelling spacers on wire

leather or fabric in slot in leg

screw-eye in top of leg

(c)

(d)

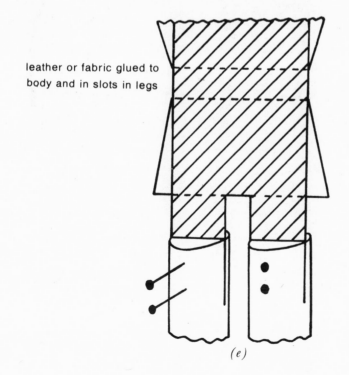

leather or fabric glued to body and in slots in legs

(e)

Dressing the marionette

Materials: soft fabrics (not too fine or the puppet will show through and not too thick or the puppet will not move freely; fabrics with large prints are not generally suitable), needles and thread, glue such as Copydex, Bostik No. 1 or UHU

1 Make paper patterns for the clothes; try the patterns for size against the puppets. (Make sure the clothes are not too tight—especially sleeves and trouser legs.)
2 Use the pattern to cut out the costume.
3 Glue or stitch the costume together. If gluing the costume, it is easy to glue the parts straight onto the puppet: start with the shirt front, collar and tie, then trousers, back and front of the coat and finally coat collar. Make the trousers from two tubes of material; leave the top seams open and glue these parts of each leg to the corresponding parts of the other trouser leg (see *Figure 55*).

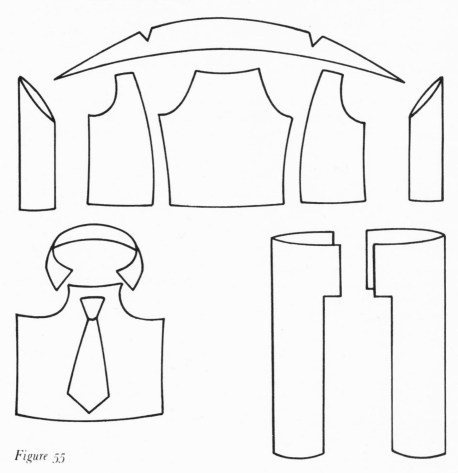

Figure 55

96

For a classical, robe-style costume:

1 Cut a circular piece of material and make four radial cuts in it as shown in *Figure 56a*.
2 Fold the material in half and stitch up the arm and side seams (*Figure 56b*).
3 Reverse the costume so that the seams are inside (*Figure 56c*).

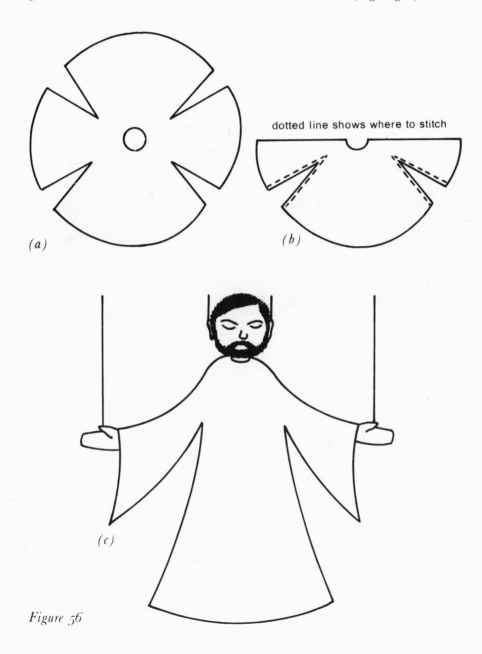

dotted line shows where to stitch

(a)

(b)

(c)

Figure 56

Stringing the marionette

General principles

Materials: carpet thread, button thread or other strong, thin thread, large needles, beeswax (if available)

Note: The marionette must be dressed before it is strung.

1   Before using strings, it is advisable to rub them with beeswax. This makes them stronger and helps to prevent fraying with use.
2   The order for stringing is: head strings, shoulder strings, hand strings, leg strings.
3   When attaching strings, first make a small hole in the carton, card, etc., push the thread through (using a needle if necessary) and tie a few knots in the string so that it cannot slip through the hole (*Figure 57a*). Seal the knot with glue.
4   If there is any danger of the thread pulling back through the hole, tie the thread to a small button (*Figure 57b*).
5   Make the strings long enough for the control to be held at elbow height when the puppet is standing on the floor (*Figure 57c*).
6   Hand strings should be just long enough to let the puppet's hands hang loosely by its sides and leg strings long enough to allow the puppet to stand straight. None of these strings should be too slack.
7   When attaching head strings and shoulder strings, they should be given approximately equal tension. To create a stoop or the appearance of aging, slacken the head strings so that the head hangs forward.
8   When all strings are attached satisfactorily to the control, tie all knots tightly and seal them with glue.
9   It is a mistake to make the control of a marionette too simple unless it has very few strings. Most strings support the puppet and tilting or turning the control achieves a wide range of movements; if the control is too simple it becomes more difficult to operate the puppet as the puppeteer must then pull individual strings to effect such movements.
10 If a marionette is dropped, the golden rule is, do not just pick it up as any loose tangles will be pulled tight into knots. Lift the control (not the puppet) gently, undoing the loose tangles carefully. Following this procedure will avoid most problems.

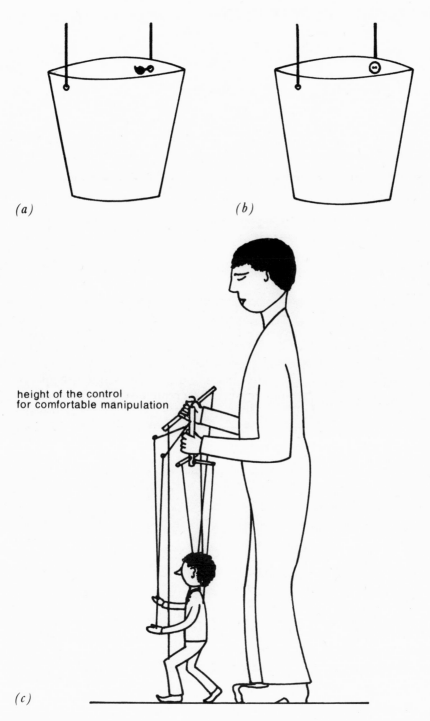

(a)

(b)

height of the control
for comfortable manipulation

(c)

Figure 57

99

Simple marionette controls

Materials: dowelling, thread

CONTROL A (*Figure 58a*)
1   Screw a hook in the centre of a dowel rod.
2   Attach the head strings near the centre of the rod and the hand strings at each end.
3   There are no leg strings. Walk the puppet by jogging the control gently.
4   Hold the control with one hand; move the rod to move head and body.
5   Use the other hand to move the puppet's hand strings.

CONTROL B (*Figure 58b*)
1   String heads and hands to the dowel rod as for control A.
2   Attach leg strings to a second dowel rod.
3   Join the two rods by a short piece of cord tied and glued to the centre of each.
4   Hold the head rod with one hand and paddle the leg bar with the other.

CONTROL C (*Figure 58c*)
1   Join two dowel rods by a short string tied to the centre of each.
2   String the head to one dowel rod.
3   String the knees to the hands and the hands to the second dowel rod.
4   Paddling the hand/leg bar lifts a hand and leg together.

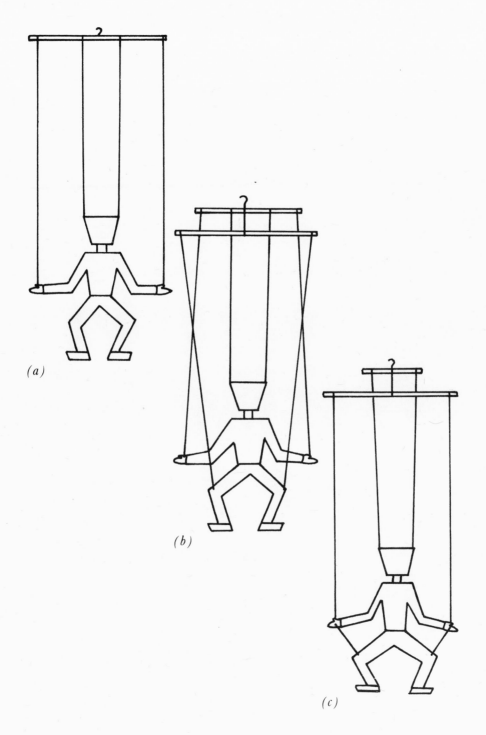

(a)

(b)

(c)

Figure 58

Horizontal control

Materials: 1 × 1 in, by 5 in long (25 × 25 mm, by 14 cm long) wooden bar, $\frac{3}{8}$ in (9 mm) or $\frac{1}{2}$ in (12 mm) diameter dowelling, one large hook, ten screw-eyes (optional), string, thread

METHOD A (*Figure 59a*)

1 The wooden bar is the main control bar. Screw a hook into the top for hanging.
2 Screw four screw-eyes into the bottom of the bar as illustrated (*Figure 59b*).
3 Cut two dowel rods, one a little wider than the head, the other wide enough to move the legs (approximately 5 or 6 in/13–15 cm).
4 Screw three screw-eyes into each dowel, one in each end and one in the middle.
5 Suspend the leg-bar from the screw-eye at the front of the control; let the rod hang about 3 in (8 cm) from the control bar.
6 Suspend the head-bar in the same way from the screw-eye next to the back of the control.
7 The other screw-eyes are for run-through strings for hands and shoulders as illustrated (*Figure 59a*).

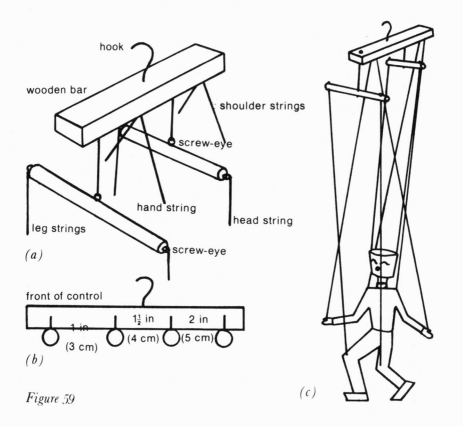

Figure 59

METHOD B (*Figure 60*)

The control is identical to that described in Method A, except that every screw-eye is removed. Strings are attached by drilling small holes through the bars, threading the strings through the holes and knotting securely. This method saves screw-eyes and avoids the possibility of strings catching on screw-eyes.

Note: With either method, a back-string (for bending from the waist) may be added if required. Attach one end to the back of the control and the other to the top of the pelvis.

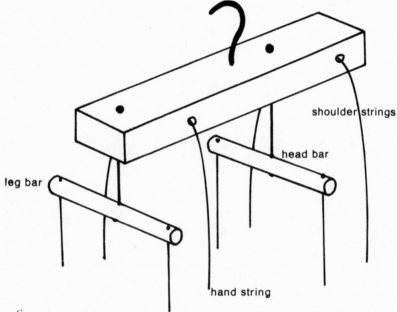

shoulder strings

head bar

leg bar

hand string

Figure 60

Manipulation
- Hold the main control with one hand.
- Tilt the control forwards to nod the puppet.
- Tilt very slightly and turn the head bar to turn the head.
- Use the other hand to move hand strings and to paddle the leg bar to walk the puppet.
- If a back-string is used, take the weight on this with one hand and lower the control with the other, so that the puppet will bend forward.

Marionette control with easy walking action

Materials: 1 × 1 in, length $5\frac{1}{2}$ in (25 × 25 mm, length 14 cm) wooden bar, three $\frac{3}{8}$ in × 7 in, 4 in and 4 in long (9 mm × 18 cm, 10 cm and 10 cm long) diameter dowels, string, thread, large hook

1   The wooden bar is the main control bar.
2   Drill two small holes, C and D (to take string) down through the control, at the middle and near the back (*Figure 61a*) and another, A, across the control near the front. Drill a $\frac{3}{8}$ in (9 cm) diameter hole, B, across the control about an inch (25 mm) behind hole.
3   Glue the 7 in (18 cm) dowel into hole B, as illustrated (*Figure 61b*).
4   Drill a small hole through each end of this rod for attaching leg strings.
5   Drill three holes through the other dowel rods for the head and shoulder bars.
6   Suspend them from the control by string, knotted at each end, as illustrated, and attach head and shoulder strings to the ends of the bars.
7   A run-through string passes through hole A; each end of the thread is tied to one of the hands.
8   A back-string may be added if required, as described for the previous control.
9   To walk the puppet, simply paddle the control from side to side.
    To bow the head, tilt the control forward.
    To move the head-bar or hand strings, use the other hand.

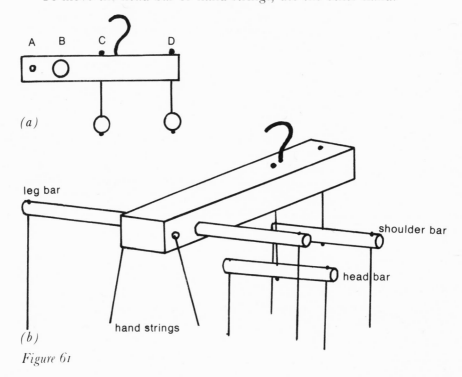

Figure 61

Upright control

Materials: two pieces of 1 × 1 in (25 × 25 mm) by 9 in and 5 in long (23 cm and 13 cm long) wood, two $\frac{3}{8}$ in (9 mm) maximum diameter by 5 in and 8 in long (13 cm and 20$\frac{1}{2}$ cm long) dowels, galvanized (coat-hanger) wire, screw-eye and two hooks (small and large)

1 The 9 in (23 cm) piece of wood is the main upright bar, the 5 in (13 cm) piece the head bar. The best method of joining them is a cross halving joint, effected by making two saw cuts halfway through each piece and then chiselling out the waste (*Figure 62a*) so that the two pieces can be interlocked, glued and screwed together (*Figure 62b*).

2 Alternatively, simply glue and screw the head bar to the upright (*Figure 62c*) or make the head bar from a piece of dowelling; drill a hole through the control and glue the head bar into it (*Figure 62d*).

3 The shoulder bar is the 5 in (13 cm) dowel. Drill a hole in the control (from back to front) below the head bar and glue the dowel into the hole so that it sticks out at the back (*Figure 62b*). This dowel must be a tight fit.

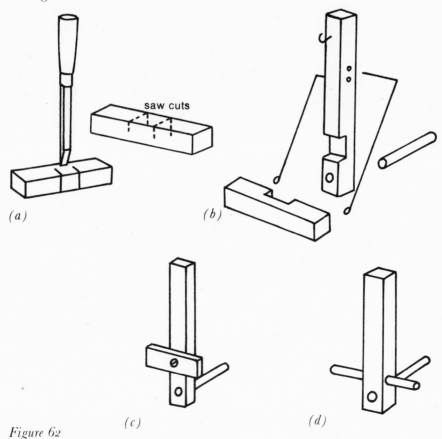

saw cuts

(a) *(b)*

(c) *(d)*

Figure 62

4   Drill two holes, one about $\frac{3}{8}$ in (9 mm) above the other, higher in the control for the hand wires.

5   To attach hand wires, first bend over one end of each wire at right angles using pliers (*Figure 63a*). Insert the long straight pieces of the wire through the holes in opposite directions, then carefully bend them over with pliers (*Figure 63b*); do not make them too tight to the upright or they will not turn freely. Cut the wires to the same length and make loops in the ends for attaching head strings (seal the closures of the loops with glue).

6   Screw a screw-eye into the centre of the long dowel which is the leg-bar and suspend this from the top of the control by a small hook (*Figure 63c*).

7   Screw a large hook into the top of the control for hanging.

8   Drill small holes through the ends of head, shoulder and leg bars for attaching the puppet's strings.

9   Add a back string (attached to the shoulder bar) if required.

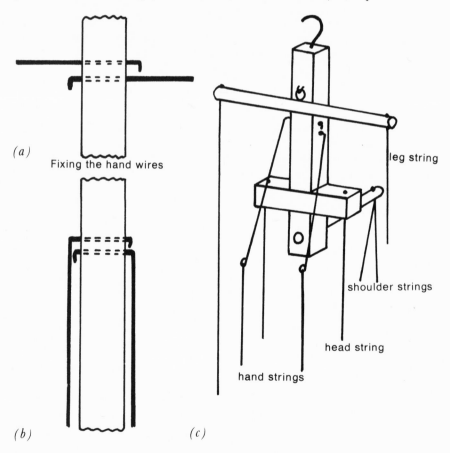

(a)
Fixing the hand wires

leg string

shoulder strings

head string

hand strings

(b)   *(c)*

Figure 63

To manipulate the upright control:

1   Hold the main control in one hand (with the little finger under the head bar if it is comfortable) and use the thumb and index finger to move the hand wires (*Figure 64*).

2   The other hand can be used to move individual hand strings for a wider range of gestures. This hand is also used to unhook and paddle the leg bar for the walking action.

3   Tilt the main control sideways to incline the head, forward to nod the head; to turn the head, tilt the control very slightly forward to take the weight on the shoulder strings, simultaneously turning the control in the appropriate direction.

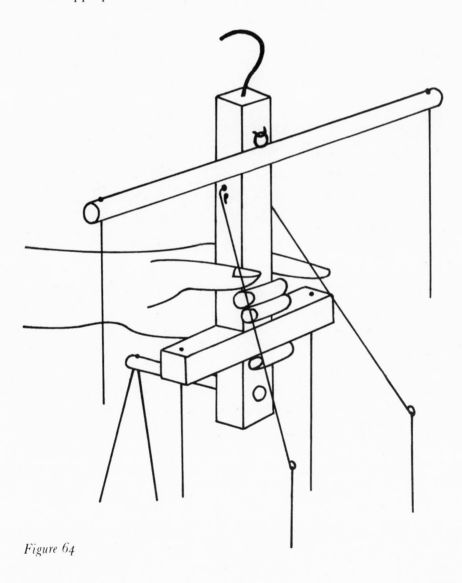

Figure 64

Animal control

Materials: 1 × 1 in (25 × 25 mm) by 6–10 in long (15–25 cm) wood, 4 in (10 cm) piece of dowelling, 6 in (15 cm) strip of wood or dowelling, one large hook, screw-eyes (optional), string, thread

1 The main control bar is the 6–10 in (15–25 cm) long piece of wood. The length depends on the size of the puppet. Fix a hook in the top.
2 To attach the leg bar, *either* glue and screw a 6 in (15 cm) strip of wood to the top of the control, near the front (*Figure 65a*) *or* drill a hole through the control, from side to side, and glue a dowel into the hole (*Figure 65b*).
3 Suspend the dowel for the head-bar from the front of the control using screw-eyes and string (*Figure 65a*) or by drilling holes through the two pieces and joining them with string knotted at each end (*Figure 65b*).
4 To attach head, leg and back strings to the control, either use screw-eyes or drill small holes through the control, as before.

Note: Most animals raise one front leg and opposite back leg together, so the string from the left back leg should be attached to the right side of the leg bar and from the right back leg to the left of the leg bar.

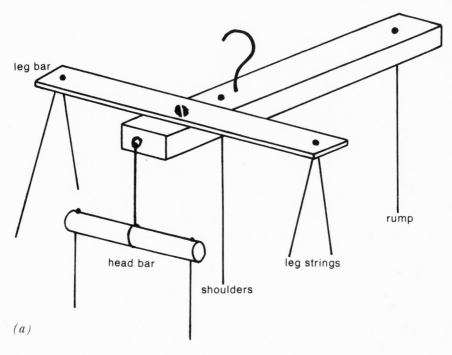

(a)

Figure 65

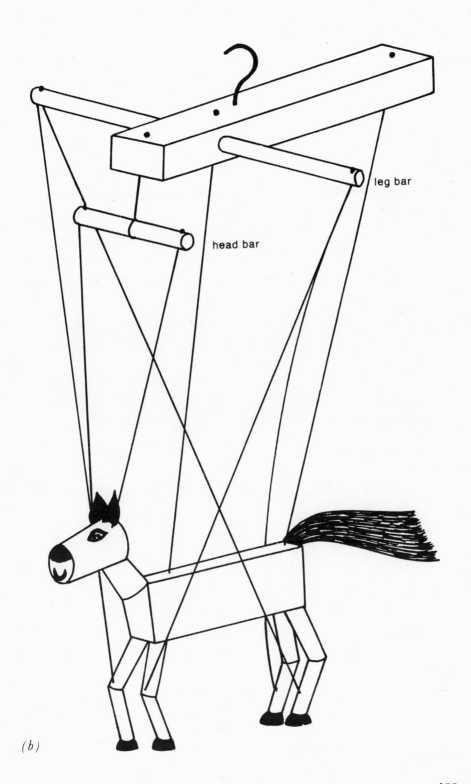

leg bar

head bar

(b)

Shadow puppet construction

Simple shadow puppet

Materials: cardboard, coat-hanger wire or a thin stick or dowel

1 It is wise to design the puppet first on paper as if it were being viewed from the side. It may be as small or as large as desired but *it must fit the screen on which it is to be used.*

2 Draw the shape on a piece of cardboard (even a cereal box will do). Contary to popular belief, the cardboard does not have to be black, nor to be painted black.

3 Carefully cut out the puppet with scissors.

4 *For control from below,* the puppet is held by a wire or rod taped to the body (*Figure 66a*).

   For control from behind, a more substantial stick is fixed to the back of the puppet by a drawing pin through the card into the end of the rod (*Figure 66b*).

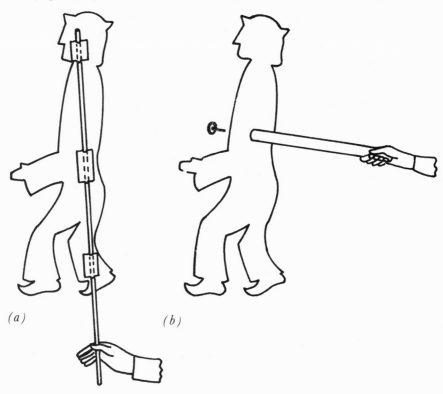

(a)   (b)

Figure 66

Articulated shadow puppet

Materials: cardboard, thread or rivet-type paper fasteners

1 Design the puppet on paper, making sure that the parts which are to be jointed are drawn overlapping (*Figure 67a*).
2 Redraw the separate parts on cardboard. (It is useful to lay carbon paper on the card, then trace the shape through from the original design.)
3 Cut out the parts (*Figure 67b*) and lay them down as if assembled to check that they overlap properly (*Figure 67c*).
4 To make the joints:
   either make a small hole in each piece of card, push a paper fastener through the holes and bend over the ends. The holes must be large enough to permit free movement—a paper punch is useful for this (*Figure 67d*).
   or with a needle insert a strong thread through both pieces of card, knot the two ends and seal the knots with glue (*Figure 67e*).

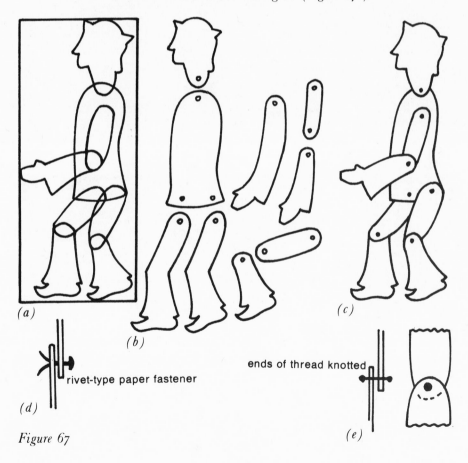

(a)

(b)

(c)

(d) rivet-type paper fastener

ends of thread knotted

(e)

Figure 67

Controlling the shadow puppet

Materials: galvanized (coat-hanger) wire, dowelling

If the puppet has a moving head, the main control bar must be fixed to the head (*Figure 68a*). Occasionally a puppet has a control fixed to the head and another to the body (*Figure 68b*), but this is awkward to hold and not recommended. If the puppet does not have a moving head (*Figure 68c*), attach the main control to the body just above the point of balance (i.e. so that there is *just a little* more weight below the rod than there is above it).

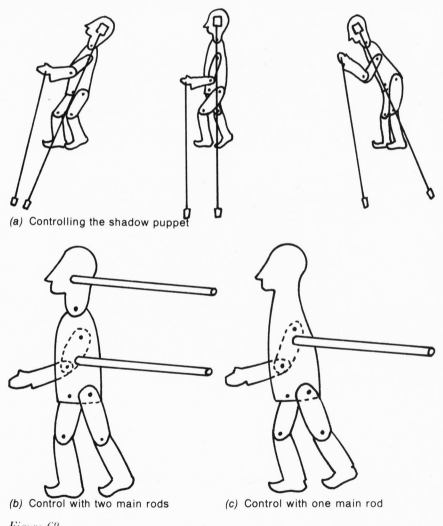

(a) Controlling the shadow puppet

(b) Control with two main rods

(c) Control with one main rod

Figure 68

Methods of fixing main controls

1 Wire or vertical rods can be fixed with sticky tape (*Figure 69a*). Masking tape is recommended.
2 Wire, with a loop in the end, can be secured by means of a strip of card glued to the puppet over the wire (*Figure 69b*). This allows the control wire to be raised and lowered for manipulation from any angle.
3 Wire with a loop in the end can be stitched to the card with strong thread (*Figure 69c*). This also permits manipulation from any angle.
4 A dowel rod can be secured by a drawing pin through the card and into the end of the rod (*Figure 69d*).
5 A dowel can be attached by means of a piece of Velcro glued securely to the card and to the end of the rod (*Figure 69c*). Simply push them together to use and pull them apart after use.

Figure 69

Arm controls

1   Many puppeteers do not use any arm controls. Considerable effective movement can be achieved by letting them hang freely and moving only one main rod (*Figure 68c*).

2   Attach a dowel rod to the hand by means of a drawing pin or Velcro (*Figures 69e and 70a*), as described above.

3   Attach a wire by making a small loop in the end (seal the closure of the loop with glue) and tying thread to the loop. With a needle, push the thread through the card and knot the end of the thread (*Figure 70b*). Umbrella spokes are particularly useful for this sort of control as they are thin and strong and already have a hole in the end, which is useful for attaching thread.

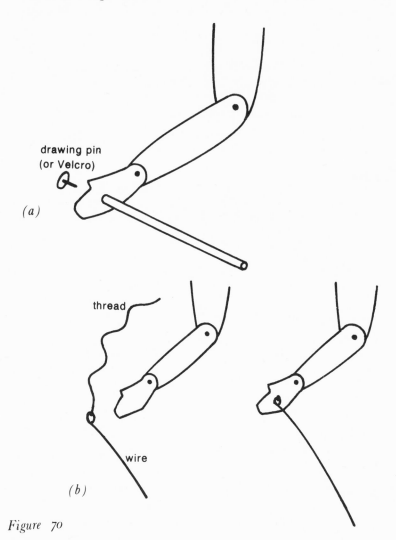

Figure 70

Legs

Legs do not usually have controls. They hang loosely from the body, but some degree of control can be effected from the way in which the main body control is moved (*Figures 68a, 68c and 71*).

Figure 71   Controlling the legs of a shadow puppet

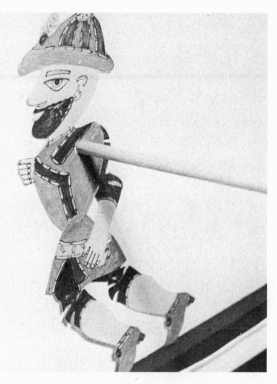

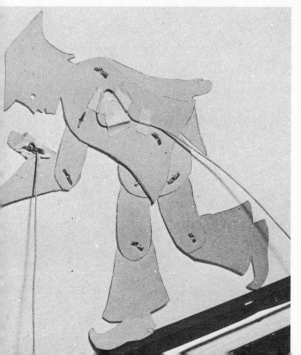

Detail and decoration in shadow puppets

Cut out designs

1 Shadow puppets need not be solid figures.
2 Detail and decoration can be cut in the figure (*Figure 72*) so that the light shines through.
3 Small scissors with sharp points are especially useful for cutting the design, and a punch is also useful.
  Take great care if using a craft knife to cut out the design and *never* cut towards the hand holding the puppet, however much easier it may appear.
4 Be careful not to cut away too much card or it will weaken the puppet.

Figure 72 Cut-out design for shadow puppets

Added decoration

Decoration can be added to the puppet by using pieces of lace, net and other loose-weave fabrics, paper doilies, etc. that will let light through and create an interesting pattern (*Figure 73*).

Figure 73 Added decoration for shadow puppets

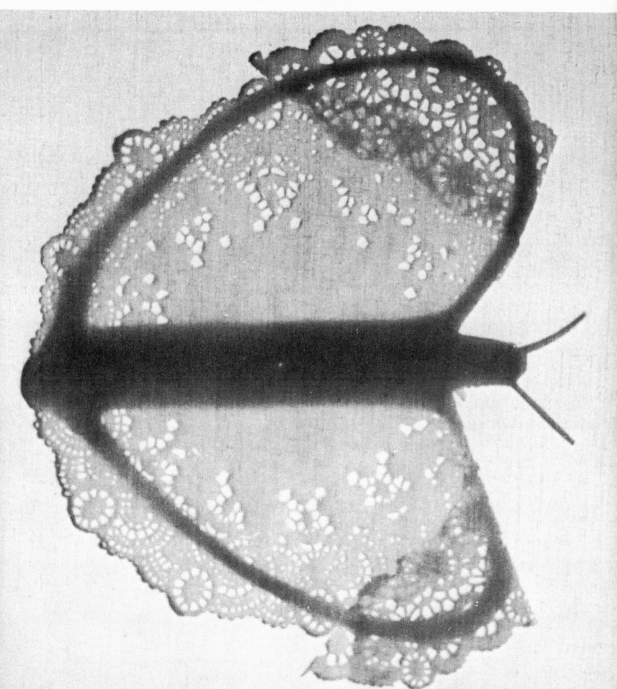

Colour with shadow puppets

Materials: cellophane paper (sweet wrappers) or coloured tissue paper or off-cuts of coloured lighting filters, sellotape (Scotch tape) or masking tape

1 Cut out the parts required to be coloured.
2 Fasten coloured tissue, cellophane, etc. over the hole by means of sticky tape.
   The colour of the paper will show through on the screen (*Figure 74*).
3 The coloured, translucent material can be used in conjunction with a lace or net fabric to create a textured and coloured effect (*Figure 75*).

Figure 74   Colour with shadow puppets

Figure 75   Colour and added decoration used together

Full-colour puppets

Materials: water-based felt pens, cooking oil, kitchen roll tissues, white card (ivory board is recommended)

1   Draw the puppet on white card (not too thick)—either a non-articulated figure or the separate parts for an articulated figure.
2   Colour the card with water-based felt pens (*not* spirit-based as the colours of these will eventually merge together and spoil the puppet).
3   Rub both sides of the card with a little cooking oil on a piece of kitchen roll until the card becomes translucent. The effect is very attractive and like oriental parchment or leather puppets.
4   Cut out the whole puppet.
5   If it is to be jointed, use the thread method described earlier but use nylon thread (fishing line) and seal the knots with clear glue.
6   To control this sort of puppet, use a horizontal rod joined by a drawing pin or Velcro.

Note: Strictly speaking, of course, these are *transparencies* rather than shadows but for convenience they are usually classed together and referred to as shadows.

Figure 76   **Full-colour puppets**

Part three
PRESENTATION TECHNIQUES

General manipulation points

Practise manipulating the puppets with each hand. See what sorts of movement suit each puppet best and try to achieve a variety of movements. Let the puppet do as much as possible for itself through its natural built-in movement.

Practise movements, as appropriate to the type of puppet and its character, such as rubbing its head, rubbing its stomach, clapping its hands, picking things up, bowing with appropriate gestures, nodding and turning the head, walking convincingly, dancing, kneeling, sitting down, standing up again, etc.

Practise entrances and exits, from wings, through doors or arches and up (imaginary) stairs in a booth to the acting level. Discover ways of moving the puppet so that it appears to be speaking (do not jerk it to every syllable of speech).

Keep the puppet walking at the same level all the time, not allowing a marionette to float or sag (and do not walk it in a sitting position). Do not hold a glove or rod puppet too high or your arm will show, nor too low or the puppet will disappear; also remember that when a glove or rod puppet is moved away from the front of a booth, it will appear to the audience to be sinking unless it is held higher.

When manipulating any type of puppet, an important rule is: *one thing at a time*. That is, make steady, deliberate movements, not a host of jiggly ones. Manipulate with a rhythm, particularly when walking the puppet, and maintain concentration—when the operator's attention wanders, it shows. Most important: *let us see the puppet think*.

Figure 77 Puppets in performance

(a) rod puppet

(b) glove puppet

(c) marionette

(d) shadow puppet

Staging adaptable to various uses

Flexible staging units

The most flexible type of staging for puppets are the units illustrated in *Figure 78* in a variety of shapes and sizes.

1 Each unit is constructed of 1 × 1 in (25 × 25 mm) or 1½ × 1½ in (38 × 38 mm) timber jointed as illustrated in *Figures 79a and b*, and held rigid by triangular plywood plates, or as in *Figure 79c*, with triangular wooden blocks.
2 Some units consist of two such rectangular frames hinged together.
3 The units may be joined in any shape required (*Figure 80*) by G-clamps.
4 The units may be covered with a suitable fabric (such as hessian) stretched across one face and stapled to the sides of the frame, or covered with card and painted.

For quick exploration and testing of ideas, tape sheets of kitchen paper or newspaper over the frames and paint the paper.

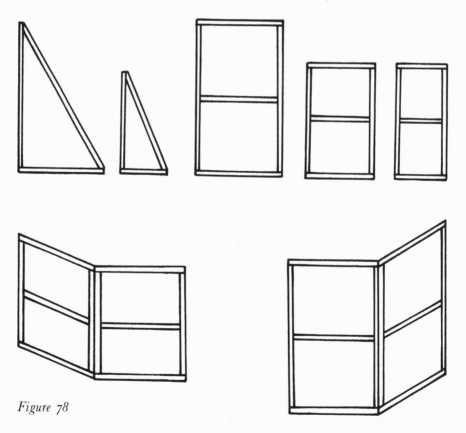

Figure 78

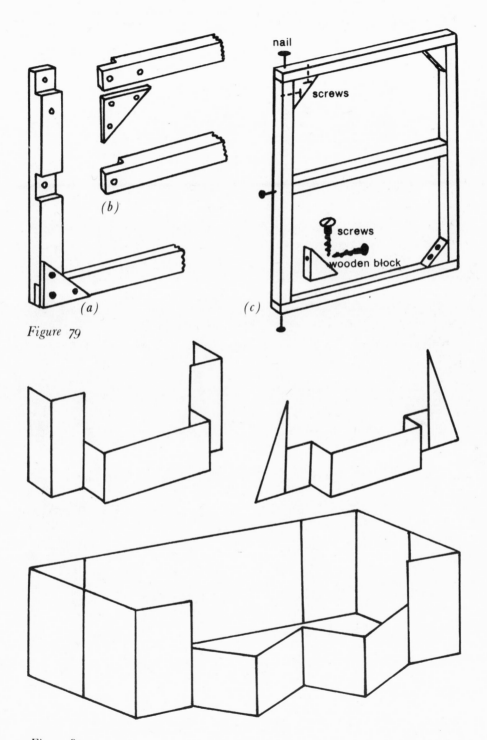

Figure 79

Figure 80

Clothes-horse theatre

Materials: three-sided clothes-horse, drapes, sheet of cotton, (three long dowel rods, two long nails, cord—all optional)

1   A clothes-horse covered in drapes is handy for a glove and rod puppet booth (*Figure 81a*) and for a back-cloth for marionettes (*Figure 81b*), provided it is not too high.
2   A cotton screen may be pinned into the top of the centre section for use as a shadow screen (*Figure 81c*).
3   For use with glove and rod puppets, a back-screen may be added if required. It helps to show the puppets and the performance to good effect (*Figure 82a*).
4   Pin or stitch a drape over a long dowel rod (*Figure 82b*).
5   Drill a hole down through the rod near each end and hammer a long nail through each hole as illustrated.
6   Drill a hole down into one end of two further dowel rods.
7   Tie these two dowels to the back uprights of the clothes-horse (*Figure 82c*).
8   Drop the nails in the ends of the curtain rail into the holes in the tops of the upright dowels (*Figures 82b and 82c*).

(a)   (b)

(c)

Figure 81

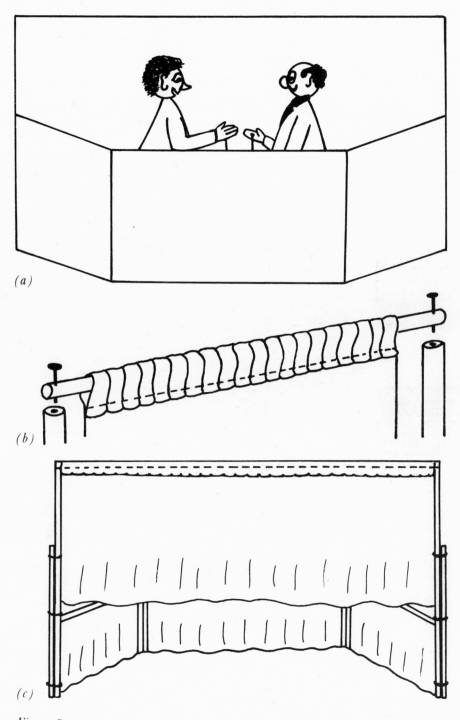

(a)

(b)

(c)

Figure 82

Simple table-top stage

Materials: old cardboard box, old strips of wallpaper or paper and paint

Making the booth

1. Cut the top and one side from a large cardboard box.
2. Open out the three sides remaining to make the booth.
3. To help to steady the booth, leave two of the bottom flaps turned inwards (stand something heavy on them if necessary) and bend the middle flap forward so that it stands out in front of the booth (*Figure 83*).
4. It is a good idea to decorate the booth with pieces of wallpaper or to cover it with plain paper which is then decorated.
5. The booth can be used for glove and rod puppets (*Figures 83a and b*) and marionettes (*Figure 84*); it can also be adapted for use as a shadow theatre (see page 148).
6. The top of the booth need not be flat and plain, of course; it may be cut to any shape required (*Figure 85a*).
7. However, it is usually advisable to keep the booth plain and adaptable and achieve variations by large scene-setting pieces held by the scenery slots described below (*Figure 85b*).

(a)

(b)

Figure 83

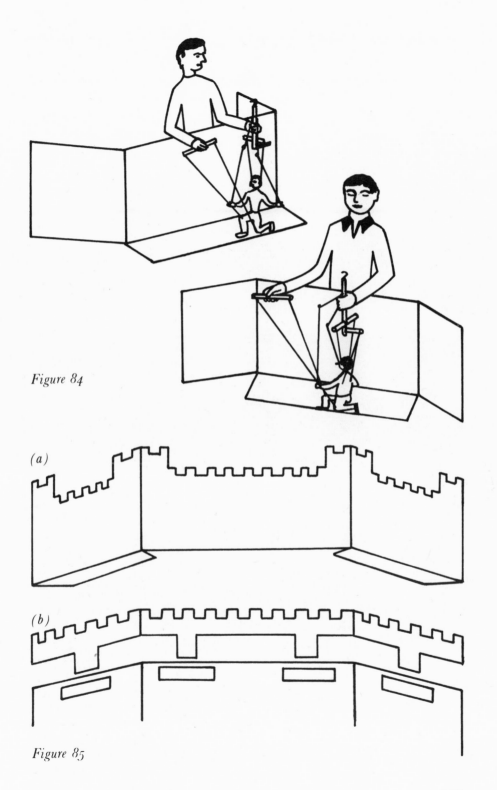

Figure 84

(a)

(b)

Figure 85

Scenery for use with glove and rod puppets

Materials: stiff cardboard, paint or fabric

1   Draw the scenery on stiff card, leaving a 2 in (5 cm) tag at the bottom (*Figure 86a*).
2   Cut out the scenery and paint it or cover it with a fabric collage.
3   To make *scenery slots*, take a strip of stiff card $1\frac{1}{2}$ in (4 cm) wide and $5\frac{1}{2}$ in (14 cm) long. Cut two 1 in (25 mm) pieces off the length.
4   Glue the 1 in (25 mm) pieces onto each end of the $3\frac{1}{2}$ in (9 cm) strip, then glue the other sides of the small pieces onto the inside of the screen, near the top (*Figure 86b*).
5   The tag on the bottom of the scenery fits into the slot between the two small pieces of card.
6   It is advisable to have a scenery slot in each corner of the front screen and one on each side piece (*Figure 86c*).

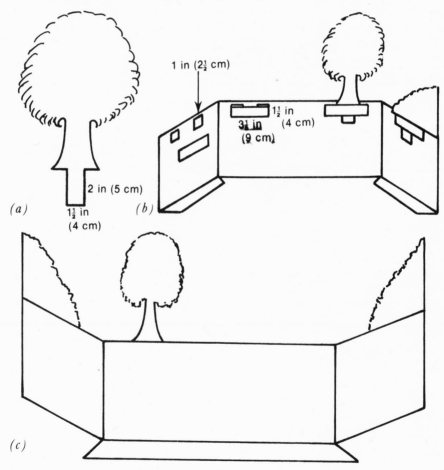

Figure 86

Proscenium theatre

Materials: 2 × 2 in (50 × 50 mm) timber, plywood, coachbolts and wing nuts, screws, curtain wire, drapes

1   This theatre consists of a framework of 2 × 2 in (50 × 50 mm) timber, screwed or bolted together as illustrated (*Figure 87*), with half-lap joints (*Figure 88*).
2   The frame is held rigid by triangular plywood plates (which may be replaced by angle struts of timber if desired).
3   The front curtain frame supports two rows of curtains, the top one overlapping the bottom one by two or three inches (five to eight centimetres).

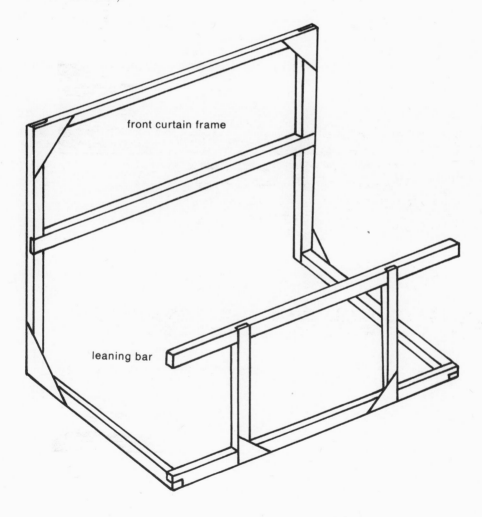

front curtain frame

leaning bar

Figure 87

4   When the lower set of curtains is opened, it becomes a marionette
    theatre (*Figure 89a*); opening the upper set reveals a glove or rod puppet
    theatre (*Figure 89b*) and a screen fixed in the opening creates a shadow
    theatre.

5   The leaning bar supports a curtain or other backcloth for marionette
    performances. For glove or rod puppet performances, use longer
    uprights so that the back-screen is raised (*Figure 89c*).

6   This arrangement permits the curtains to be opened as wide as desired
    for each performance, so the size of the acting area can be altered.

7   The curtains hang from a curtain wire (which has been omitted from
    the illustration for clarity).

8   They are opened and closed by a long cord (*Figure 89d*) which is tied to
    the inner rings of the curtains (marked X).

9   The cord is threaded through the curtain rings. It passes over a hook or
    screw-eye in the upright at one end and over two hooks in the upright
    at the other end.

10 The ends of the cord are weighted; pull one end to open the curtains
    and the other end to close them.

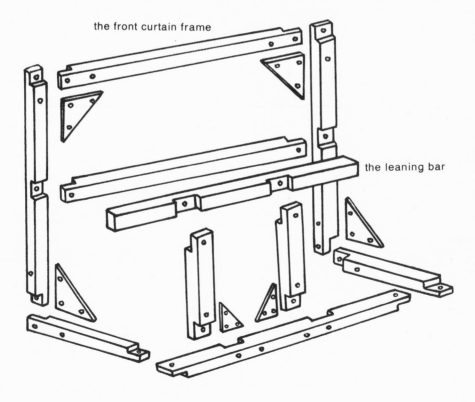

the front curtain frame

the leaning bar

Figure 88

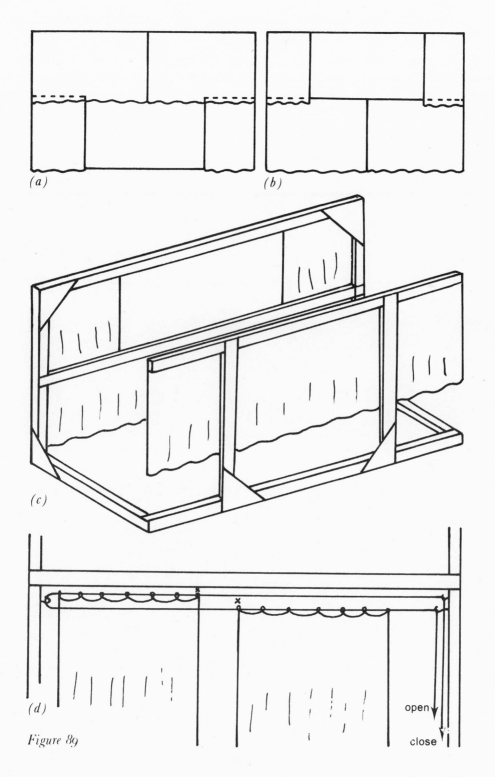

(a)

(b)

(c)

(d)

open

close

Figure 89

Glove and rod puppet presentation

Screen for glove and rod puppets

Materials: A side of a large cardboard box, sticks and other trimmings, tape

1 The screen may be any shape, representing any object; the ship illustrated is simply an example (*Figures 90a and b*).
2 Draw the shape required on the side of a cardboard box and cut it out and paint and decorate the side to face the audience.
3 To support the screen, cut out four right-angled triangles, bend over one side of each, as illustrated, and glue these edges onto each side of the screen.
4 Fold the triangles flat to pack away the screen.
5 Add any trimmings or details (such as the masts taped onto this ship) as required.
6 Stand the screen on a table for operation.
7 Alternatively, a larger screen may be used with a curtain tacked to the bottom of it with strong thread. Use cords through the card to tie each end of the screen to a chair for support (*Figures 91a and b*).

Model booth

Materials: large cardboard boxes

1 Make a large model from cardboard boxes to serve as the booth.
2 The operators are hidden inside the model as they operate the puppets (*Figure 92*).
   This method allows viewing from any position around the booth.

132

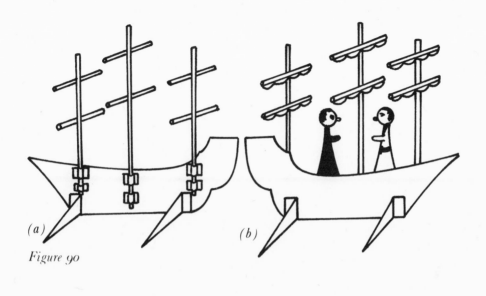

Figure 90

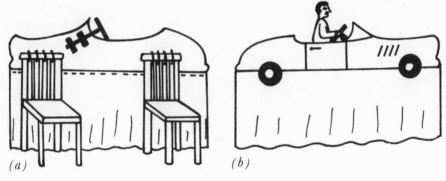

Figure 91

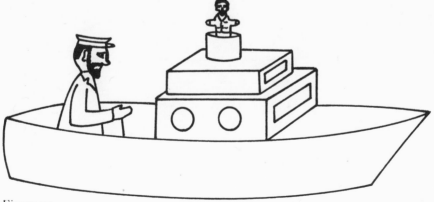

Figure 92

Open booth

Materials: 2 × 2 in (50 × 50 mm) timber, plywood, coachbolts with wing nuts, hinges, screws, curtain wire, drapes

1   The dimensions for the booth will depend on individual requirements, including the height of the operators. It consists basically of a front curtain frame, adjustable in height, and a back screen (*Figure 93a*), but it can be extended in width and may incorporate a shadow screen (*Figure 93b*).

2   The basis of the frame is three units (*Figure 93c*) made in the same way as the flexible staging units described earlier (page 122) and hinged together. A shadow screen may be built into the centre of the long middle unit.

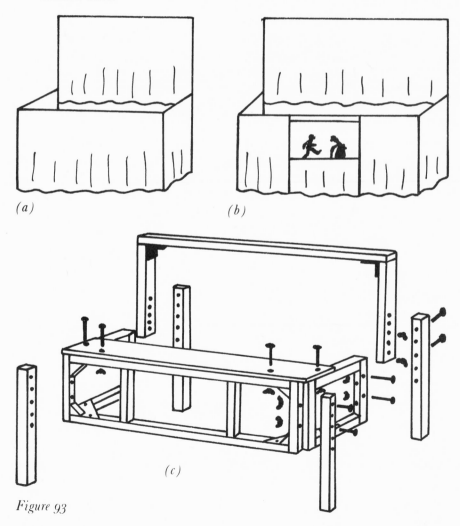

(a) *(b)*

(c)

Figure 93

3 Alternatively, the frame may be made from two hinged units, bolted together (*Figure 93d*), so that they may be separated and another unit bolted between them to extend the stage (*Figure 93e*); this added unit may also hold a shadow screen.

4 A playboard (or shelf along the acting level) may be needed; it is made from a plywood plate which bolts onto the frame (*Figure 93c*).

5 Two small plywood shelves, cut to fit the corners of the booth (*Figure 93f*), bolt onto the bottom of the frame in the front corners (*Figure 93c*); these are very handy for props and they hold the corners rigid.

6 The booth is supported by four legs which bolt onto the four corners (*Figure 93c*). If the booth is extended, two extra legs should be bolted to the inside of the added unit (*Figure 93e*). Drill a series of equally spaced holes in the legs so that the booth may be adjustable in height.

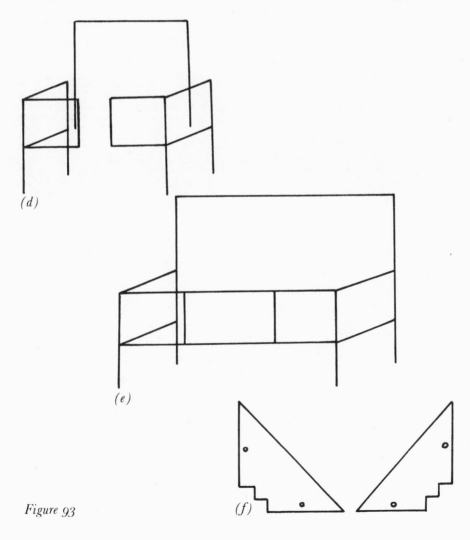

(d)

(e)

Figure 93   (f)

7   The back frame consists of three lengths of timber hinged together and bolted to the back of the main frame (*Figure 93c*). To this may be added drapes (*Figure 93a*) or a back-screen cut from plywood or hardboard (*Figure 93g*) and bolted to the timber. Alternative back-cloths are described in the section on 'Marionette presentation'.

8   Add drapes to the main framework, securing them with tapes or Velcro (glued to the framework and stitched to the curtains). In order to allow for changes in height, secure a separate small curtain to the bottom of the booth with curtain wire (*Figure 93h*).

9   A further curtain wire fixed to the inside of the main frame may be used for hanging up glove puppets when not in use (*Figure 93i*).

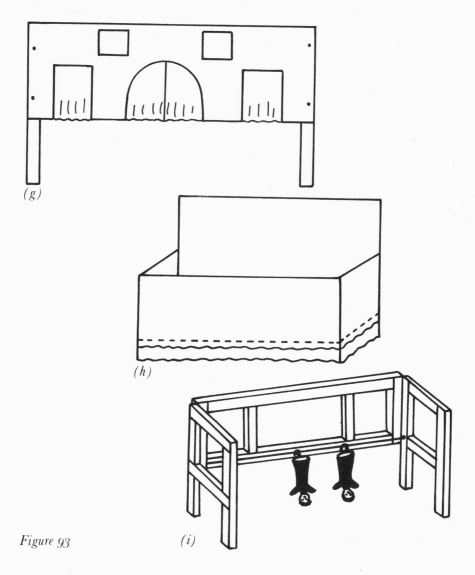

(g)

(h)

Figure 93   (i)

Scenery and props

Materials: selections from plywood, hardboard, cardboard, timber, dowels, screws, bolts and wing nuts, screw-eyes, thread, G-clamps

Scenery and a scenery slot

1   Scenery may be cut from plywood, hardboard or strong card. Leave a tag on the bottom (*Figure 94a*) or glue a plywood tag onto cardboard scenery (*Figure 94b*).
2   The tags on the scenery fit into a scenery slot: glue two pieces of plywood to the main frame (*Figure 94c*), then glue another strip of plywood on top of these two pieces to form a slot (*Figure 94d*). Secure it further with screws.
3   Drill a hole through the plywood and the main frame.
4   Stand the scenery tag in the slot and drill through the tag too.
5   The scenery is secured by a dowel peg through the holes. The dowel is attached to the framework by screw-eyes and thread.

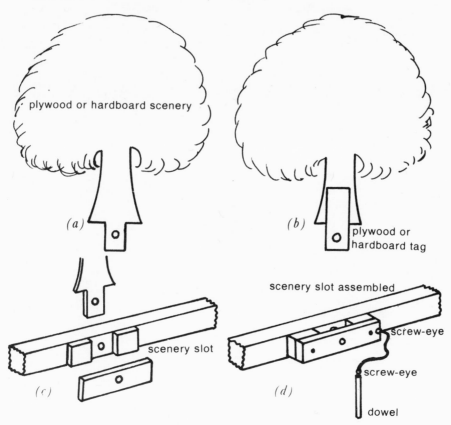

plywood or hardboard scenery

(a)

(b) plywood or hardboard tag

scenery slot assembled

scenery slot

screw-eye

screw-eye

(c)

(d)

dowel

Figure 94

Sliding slot scenery

1 The 'slide' is a strip of plywood attached vertically to the main frame (*Figure 95a*).
2 The sliding slot consists of four small pieces of plywood glued between three plywood strips (*Figures 95b and c*), creating two slots.
3 The vertical slide fits into one slot and the scenery tag (*Figures 95a and b*) fits into the other.
4 A hole is drilled through the sliding slot, the top of the vertical slide and the scenery tag; a dowel peg is used to secure the scenery in place, as described above.
5 To bring scenery into view, leave the sliding slot at the bottom of the slide, insert the scenery in the slot, steadily raise the sliding slot to the top of the slide and insert the dowel (*Figure 95d*).

This method is the most satisfactory for introducing scenery smoothly during a performance and the puppeteer's hands do not come into view.

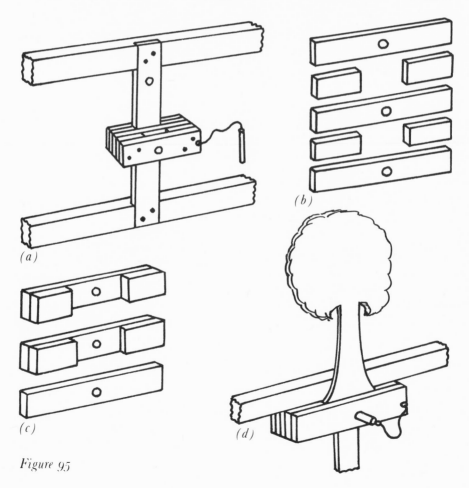

(a)

(b)

(c)

(d)

Figure 95

Other means of fastening scenery and props

1 Cardboard, plywood and hardboard items of scenery may be glued and tacked to a block of wood and then bolted or clamped to the frame of the booth or the playboard (*Figures 96a and b*).

2 Props may be stood on the playboard or secured by means of a large spring clip (*Figure 96c*).

3 Scenery and props attached to dowel rods may be moved around—or even danced and manipulated as puppets. In order to stand such items on a playboard, the playboard will need to be slotted (*Figure 97*).

4 For free-standing scenery, tie or tape the rods to a chair or other suitable fixtures (*Figure 98*).

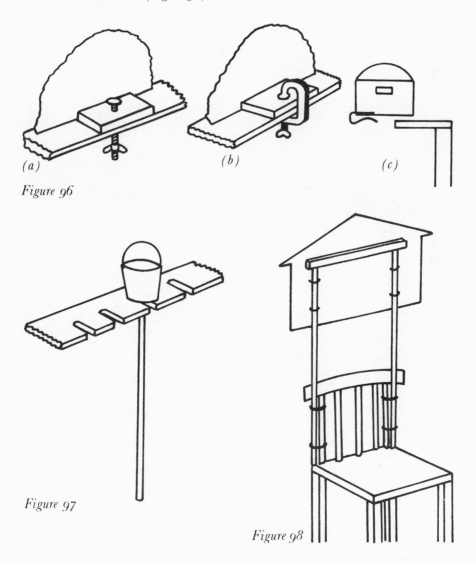

(a)   (b)   (c)

Figure 96

Figure 97

Figure 98

Marionette presentation

Performing without a stage

One can operate marionettes standing on the floor or on a raised platform (which is preferable for viewing), with no other staging (*Figure 99*).

An improvized backcloth

1   A simple backcloth may be improvised by attaching a drape to a long rod (window pole, cross-bar from a jumping stand, etc.).
2   Support the rod by resting the ends on desks or chairs (*Figure 100*).
3   Alternatively, any form of available screen, display unit, etc. of an appropriate height may be used.

Note: The rod that supports the backcloth for marionettes is called a leaning bar.

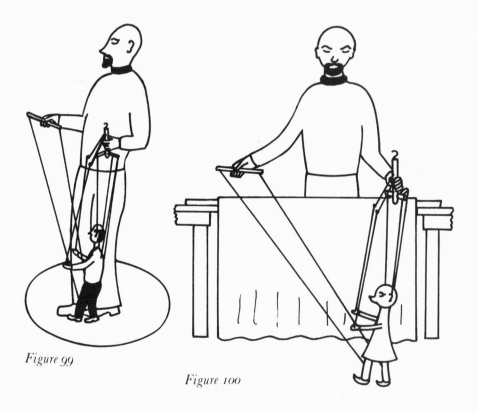

Figure 99

Figure 100

Basic open stage

Materials: $1\frac{1}{2} \times 1\frac{1}{2}$ in $(38 \times 38$ mm$)$ timber, plywood, screws, hinges, cord, drapes

1 A simple version of the open stage consists of three frames, hinged together and covered with drapes (*Figure 101*). These are constructed as described under 'Flexible staging units' (page 122), and the 'Open booth' (see page 134) may be used without the legs.
2 The framework stands on the floor and a cord across each corner prevents it from opening too far.

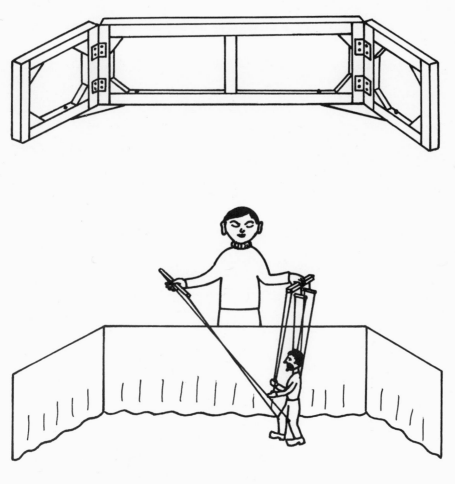

Figure 101

More elaborate open stage

Materials: 2 × 2 in (50 × 50 mm) timber, plywood, screws, coachbolts and wing nuts, dowel rods, towel rail supports, drapes

1   .A more elaborate open stage is constructed from 2 × 2 in (50 × 50 mm) timber, screwed or bolted together with half-lap joints and held rigid by triangular plywood plates (*Figure 102b*).
2   It consists of a backcloth, two wings and a back-frame (perchery) for hanging up the puppets (*Figure 102a*).
3   The perchery is a rod (or rods joined in the centre by metal tubing if necessary), the ends of which fit into holes in the side uprights; it is supported in the centre by towel rail supports which are screwed to the cross-bar (*Figure 102c*).
4   Attach drapes by means of tapes, curtain wire or Velcro (glued to the wood and sewn to the curtains).

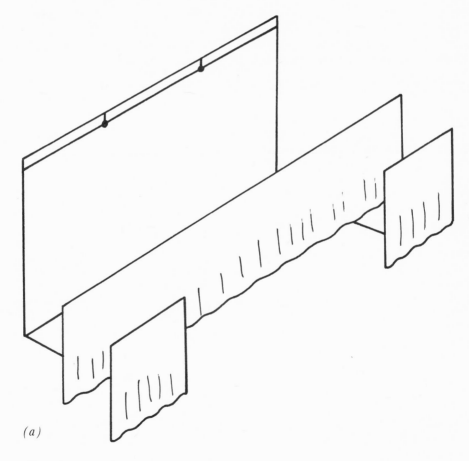

(a)

Figure 102

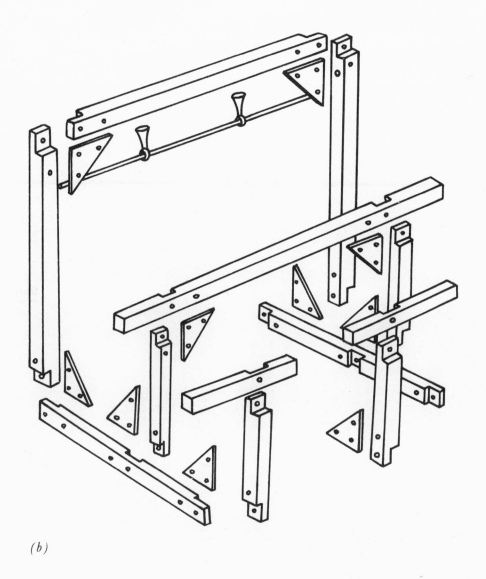

(b)

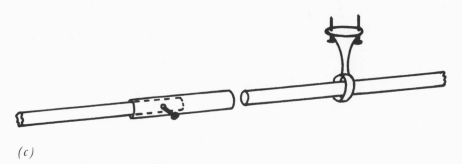

(c)

Scenery and props

Backcloths

1 A plain, draped backcloth may be used for any type of show. A fairly dark, neutral colour is best.
2 The scene may be painted on a long strip of paper (the back of an unused strip of wallpaper is good for this). Pin or tape the paper to the leaning bar. Try using sponges and other materials to obtain a textured finish.
3 A more durable scene may be made by painting on a piece of unbleached calico (*Figure 103*).
4 A collage (material picture) makes a good back-scene. Use an old piece of material or curtain as the base and glue or stitch the materials onto it (*Figure 104*).
5 The batik process used on white cotton is a splendid technique for puppet scenery (*Figure 105*):
   (i)   Heat the wax and paint it onto all parts of the fabric to remain white.
   (ii) Soak the material in cold water dye of a chosen colour x, in accordance with the manufacturer's instructions.
   (iii) Rinse and hang to dry. Then add wax to those parts required to stay colour x, and dye the material colour y.
   (iv) Repeat the process as before and continue for all colours required. Finally, boil the wax out of the material.
   Obviously the ordering of colours is important, starting with the lightest and taking into account the effect of each new colour on the previous colours and vice versa.

Figure 103   Scenery painted on paper or unbleached calico

Figure 104   Fabric collage

Figure 105   Batik backcloth

Sets and props

1 Props and sets may be made from cardboard boxes, corrugated card, etc (*Figure 106a*).
2 *Figure 106b* shows a set made of corrugated and flat card used in front of a painted backcloth.
3 Free-standing items of scenery should be supported securely. A piece of cut-out cardboard scenery may be pinned or nailed to a block of wood (*Figure 106c*) and the scenery painted or finished with a fabric collage.
4 Alternatively, the scenery may be cut with the addition of base and side flaps which are then glued together (*Figure 106d*). A weight (e.g. a can containing stones) is stood on the base to secure the scenery.

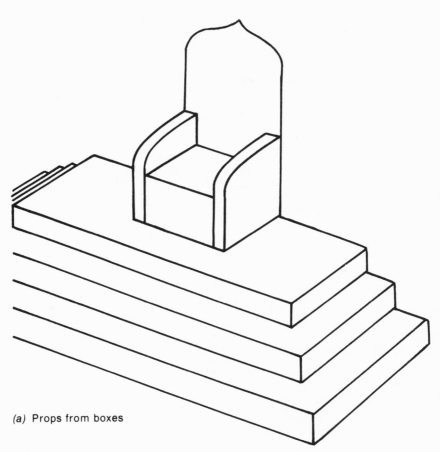

(a) **Props from boxes**

Figure 106

(b) Cardboard in front of a painted backcloth

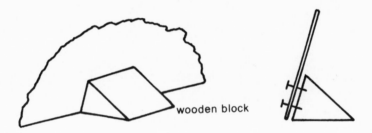

wooden block

(c) Cardboard scenery nailed or pinned to a wooden block

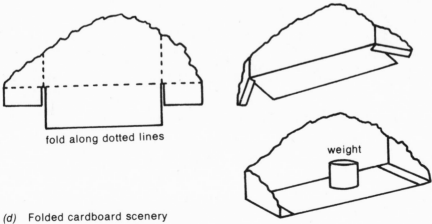

fold along dotted lines

weight

(d) Folded cardboard scenery

Shadow puppet presentation

Shadow screens

1 Shadow screens may be made from any translucent material.
2 It is possible to use greaseproof paper but there is always the danger of it tearing.
3 White cotton is the most suitable cheap material to use.
4 A light coloured cotton may be used but this is not usually suitable if coloured effects with the puppets or with the lighting are to be used.

Shadow theatre made from a cardboard box

Materials: Cardboard box, cotton sheeting, masking tape

1 The basic frame is made in the same way as described for a booth for glove and rod puppets (page 126), by cutting off the top and one side of a cardboard box (*Figure 107a*).
2 From the centre section cut a hole for the screen. Leave at least four inches between the bottom of the screen and the bottom of the box (*Figure 107b*).
3 Fasten the screen over the inside of the hole using glue or masking tape. (Stretch the fabric taut so that it does not sag or wrinkle.) (*Figure 107c*).
4 From the side cut off earlier, cut a decorative top-piece to hide the operator. For a shadow theatre alone, glue this to the frame above the screen (*Figure 107d*). If the theatre is to be used for glove and rod puppets as well, attach the top piece by means of the scenery slots (see page 153).
5 Decorate the theatre as desired.

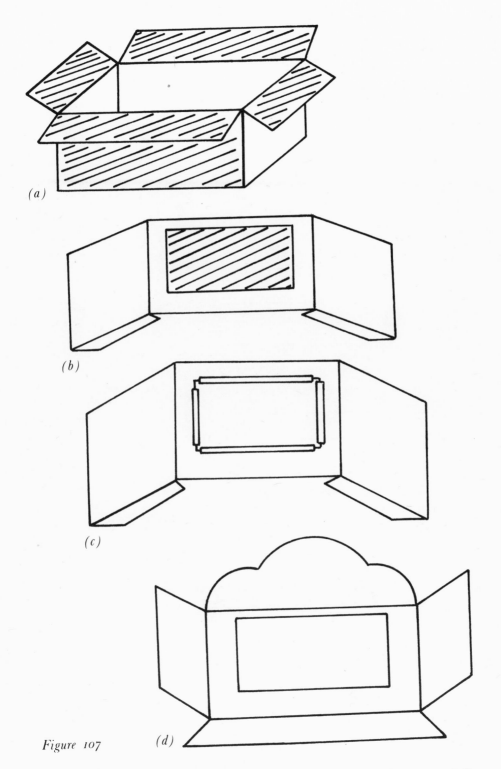

(a)

(b)

(c)

Figure 107　　*(d)*

Scenery for the shadow screen

1 Very often, shadow plays have no scenery. Every piece of scenery cuts down on the space for action.

2 A little scenery, just to set the scene, may be placed on either side of the screen, *or* a single small piece in the centre. It is not a good idea to have both (*Figure 108a*).

3 A complete scenery set may be cut from a large piece of cardboard (*Figure 108b*).

4 Always leave an extra piece of card on the bottom of the scenery, and on the side where appropriate, to help to fix the scenery against the screen.

5 Colour and detail may be introduced into the scenery, as with the puppets (pages 116–118) (*Figure 108c*).

6 The shape of the whole screen may be altered by using a scenery set which surrounds the screen and establishes the different shape (*Figure 109*).

7 Full colour translucent scenery, made in the same way as full colour shadow puppets (page 119) will allow figures behind it to be visible.

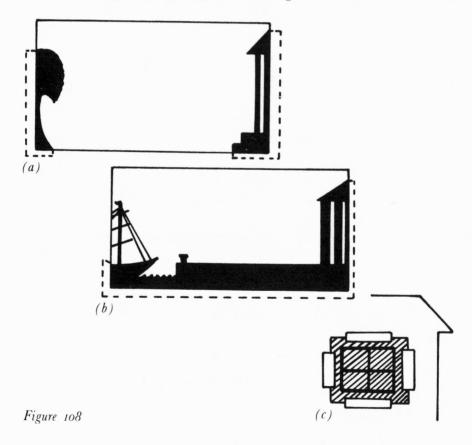

Figure 108

(a)

(b)

(c)

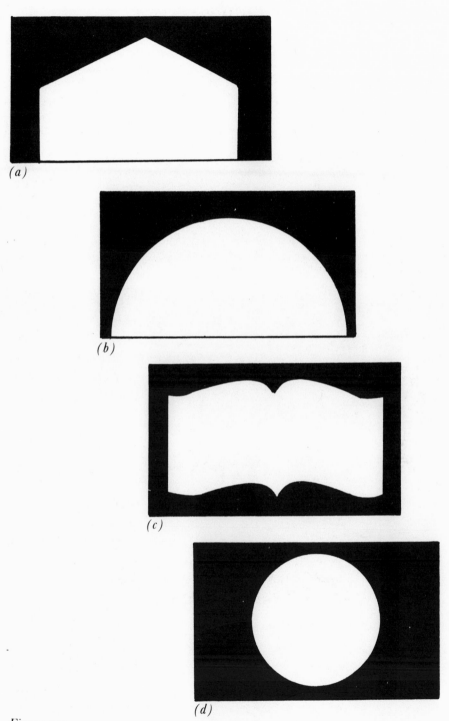

(a)

(b)

(c)

(d)

Figure 109

Securing scenery to the screen

The clothes-horse shadow theatre

1   If a clothes-horse is used to hold the screen, scenery may be attached to the edges of the screen with paper clips, a bulldog clip or drawing pins (*Figure 110a*).

2   Items to stand in the centre of the screen may be suspended by a fine thread from a paper clip attached to the top of the screen (*Figure 110b*) or it may be part of a larger scenery set, secured at the sides and bottom of the screen.

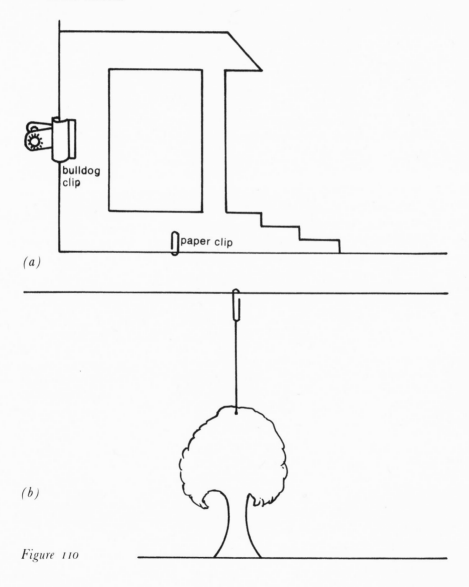

Figure 110

The cardboard shadow theatre

1 Cut six strips of cardboard as shown in *Figure 111a*.
2 Glue the three narrow strips along the sides and bottom of the screen (leaving a space of $1\frac{1}{2}$ in (38 mm) between the strips and the screen) as in *Figure 111b*.
3 Glue the wide strips on top of the narrow ones so that the wide ones almost touch the edge of the screen (*Figure 111c*).
4 Slip the scenery into the slots created thus (*Figure 111d*).

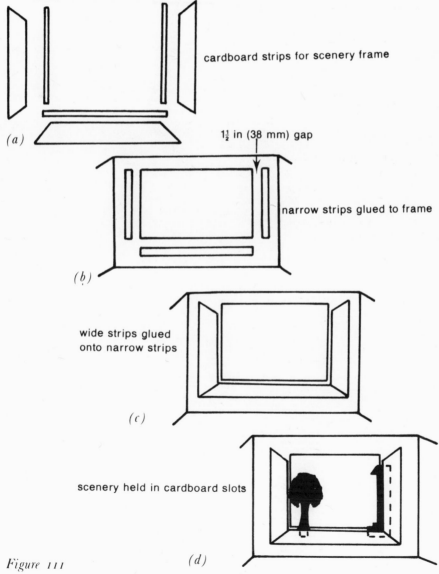

cardboard strips for scenery frame

(a)

$1\frac{1}{2}$ in (38 mm) gap

narrow strips glued to frame

(b)

wide strips glued
onto narrow strips

(c)

scenery held in cardboard slots

Figure 111   (d)

Picture frame shadow screen

Materials: an old picture frame, strip of wood, strip of plywood, card, two angle brackets, long strip of timber, screws, drapes, G-clamp (optional)

1 Secure the picture frame to the strip of wood (the base) with strong angle brackets (*Figure 112a*).
2 Secure a cotton screen to the inside of the frame with drawing pins or a staple gun.
3 Screw the long strip of timber to the inside top edge of the frame and attach the drapes to this (*Figure 112b*) by means of a curtain wire or Velcro.
4 The base will hold the screen upright but, for extra steadiness, the base may be clamped to a table top (using suitable protection for the table).
5 To hold scenery, glue onto the frame three pieces of card and onto these glue a strip of plywood to create grooves into which scenery may be slotted.

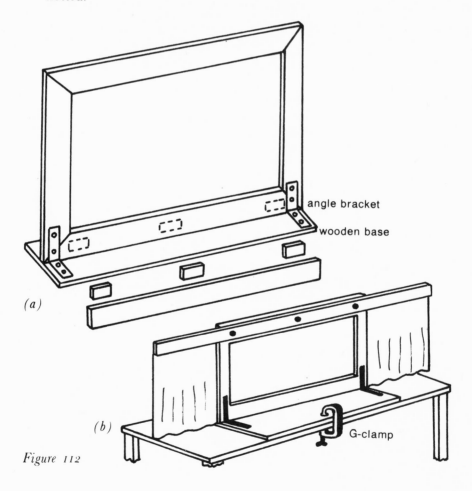

angle bracket

wooden base

(a)

(b)

G-clamp

Figure 112

Larger shadow theatre

Materials: $1\frac{1}{2} \times 1\frac{1}{2}$ in (38×38 mm) timber, length of wood 9 in (23 cm) wide, plywood, screws, coachbolts and wing nuts, cotton screen, drapes

1 The front curtain frame consists of $1\frac{1}{2} \times 1\frac{1}{2}$ in (38×38 mm) timber screwed together with half-lap joints (*Figure 113a*).
2 It screws on to a lower strip which is secured to the base board by screws through the bottom of the board.
3 The screen is pinned or stapled to the inside of the frame. The bottom of the screen is secured to a cross-bar which is attached to the frame by bolts with wing nuts.
4 Slots cut in the uprights (made by drilling a series of holes close together) allow this cross-bar to be adjusted so that the screen may be kept taut. This cross-bar also provides a ledge on which puppets can walk.
5 Attach drapes by means of a curtain wire or Velcro (glued to the frame and stitched to the drapes as in *Figures 113b and c*). The small curtain below the screen is suspended from a curtain wire fixed between the two uprights.
6 Scenery is inserted in the space between the screen and the lower cross-bar.

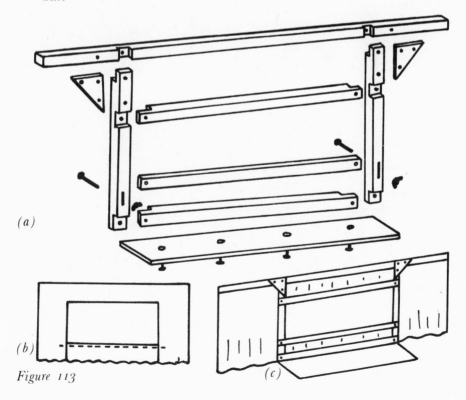

(a)

(b)

(c)

Figure 113

Lighting the puppet theatre

Is it worth using lighting?

A professional puppeteer who has many school engagements was attending one of my courses intended primarily for teachers. When the lighting session began, he said that he never used lighting because he found it too expensive and too much trouble when setting up quickly; moreover, he seemed to manage without it quite successfully.

The demonstration was simple:

1 A few puppets were manipulated in a booth with only the room lighting on (it was a darkish day in winter). The puppets were visible but did not stand out against the background and while attention on the stage was satisfactory, it was not completely focused in that it was still possible to be aware of the surroundings.

2 The puppets were manipulated with the addition of two or three small spotlights but with the room lighting kept on. With this change, attention was already focused more closely on the action, and the modelling and characterization of the puppets was enhanced.

3 The room lighting was switched off, leaving only the spotlights. Attention was now sharply focused, modelling enhanced and atmosphere created.

The following week the puppeteer arrived with a few display spotlights he had just purchased for his show. The third week he arrived and announced that he had given his first performance using lighting. The setting up had aroused interest and he was struck by a child's remark as the stage lighting was turned on and the house lights off: 'Oh, it's a *real* puppet show!'

The effort is well worth it; effective lighting can be achieved quite cheaply and the setting up time can be minimal, although obviously lighting will not be appropriate for some types of classroom use.

Figure 114 A rod puppet viewed under different lighting conditions

(a) plain daylight

(b) a single, front-of-house light

(c) two side lights

(d) a mixture of lights

Lighting for three-dimensional puppets

If artificial lighting is used, it is essential that it is bright enough. It should not call undue attention to itself and should be placed so as not to dazzle the audience.

The lighting used will depend on what is already available and what can be afforded but a minimum of two lights, preferably three, is recommended, although obviously more are desirable. Three allows two side lights to be balanced by a central light; more lights increase the scope for creating atmosphere and effects such as illuminating backcloths, casting shadows for dramatic impact, etc.

Ordinary light bulbs are not generally satisfactory; the light they provide is not usually adequate, nor directional and they often create a lot of glare. Reflector spotlights are far preferable. They may be either of the types of reflector spotlight illustrated in *Figures 115a and b*. They can be held in a photographic reflector which clips onto any fixture on, or separate from, a booth (*Figure 115a*) in modern display or home lighting fitments (*Figure 115b*) which may be purchased with a base to stand as it is or with a fitment to enable it to be secured in any position. Plain or coloured Attralux reflector spotlights, which are held by these latter fitments, are very effective and can be used without creating glare.

Many schools for older children will have a certain amount of stage lighting such as the profile spotlight illustrated (*Figure 115c*). These are highly desirable as the beam is variable in shape and size and the lights also accommodate colour filters.

Variable control of lighting may be effected at a very modest price by home dimmer switches (*Figure 115d*) but care must be taken not to overload the dimmers. Properly connected and earthed, these are perfectly safe for children to handle.

(a) Photax Interfit reflector with clip-on frame and reflector spotlight

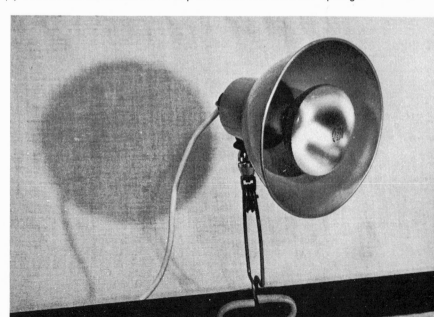

Figure 115

(b) Reflector spotlights (display lighting or home spotlight)

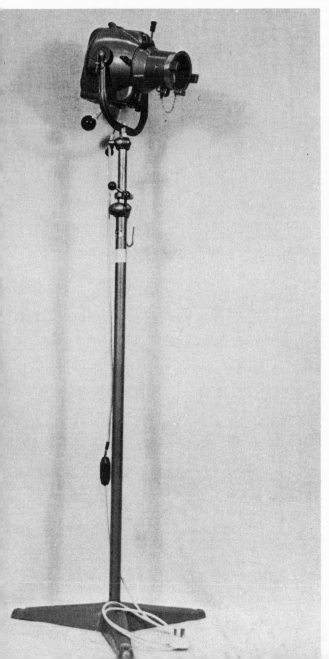

(d) dimmer switch

(c) Rank Strand Electric profile
spotlight on telescopic stand

Figure 115

159

Lighting the shadow screen

Performing by daylight

1   Ordinary daylight will give sufficient light for a shadow show (*Figure 116*).
2   Set up the screen between the window and the audience.
3   Bright sunlight will give a stronger shadow but the performer must be careful not to cast his own shadow on the screen.
4   Ordinary diffused lighting allows the performer to stand behind the screen without casting his shadow on it. Only the puppets held against the screen will create shadows.

Figure 116

Artificial lighting for shadow play

If artificial lighting is to be used, it should always be a single light. Two lights will give a blurred shadow.

1 A torch (flashlight) or bicycle lamp will give sufficient light for a small table-top screen. Stand it on the table behind the screen, taking care that the shadows of the operator's hands are not cast on the screen (*Figure 117*).

2 An angle-poise lamp or even an old table lamp without its shade will give a good light for shadow play (*Figure 118*).

3 An overhead light can be used but it is not as satisfactory as the other methods (*Figure 119*).

4 An overhead projector (*Figure 120*) or slide projector produces a very sharp shadow which grows larger as the puppet is moved away from the screen towards the light. Overhead projectors also permit images, scenery, etc. to be drawn on transparencies and projected onto the screen.

Figure 117

angle-poise lamp

Figure 118

overhead light

Figure 119

overhead projector

Figure 120

Part four
DEVELOPING PUPPETRY ACTIVITIES

Examples of projects

The first section of this book explained the nature of puppetry in education, illustrating how it might be incorporated into the school curriculum and the benefits to be derived from it. There are, however, many teachers who recognize the benefits but who find it difficult to identify possibilities for utilizing puppets to advantage within a specific curriculum area, or to draw other learning experiences from puppetry activities. This section seeks to help by providing various examples of how such activities have been developed with children.

It is unfortunate that many projects which use puppetry in a 'language development programme' or 'reading programme' are, more often than not, simply texts prescribing encounters or playlets in which a small child, cat, dog or similar character is taken through a series of exercises, for example in phonics. These exercises with puppets are usually trivial and tedious, surviving only through the popularity of puppetry; they fail to take account of the meaning of 'education', of advances in our understanding of how children learn, the nature of the reading process and the various approaches possible. The same is true of puppet activities in mathematics, religious studies, ecology projects, etc. This is a worrying development because it is being taken up by many teachers with a great lack of discernment. Such programmes are carefully organized and the stages methodically detailed, so that they seem to be efficient and effective, but the teacher fails to see that in terms of real educational content, they are sadly lacking. Too often, objectives are ill-defined or of dubious validity.

It cannot be emphasized too strongly that the activities in question should aim to meet the child's needs as identified by the teacher and relate to his level of understanding, physical abilities, etc.; it is not always possible to predict what aspect of the work will capture the child's interest or imagination. A detailed scheme of work to which the teacher adheres religiously is therefore not particularly helpful. What is most useful is understanding puppets and puppetry, and carefully cultivating the habit of thinking about the possibilities for learning experiences they offer, so that these can be readily identified as they arise.

Cornerstones of puppetry in education are careful thought and good organization within a flexible framework, plus an understanding of each child's development, needs and interests. The child's initiatives and his response to the teacher's provision will guide the teacher in planning subsequent learning experiences. It must be remembered too, that often one does not embark upon a puppetry activity in order to teach a specific concept but, in the course of the activity, many opportunities will arise which either challenge or confirm the child's experience—that is, opportunities to stimulate further learning or reinforce previous learning.

The following examples are therefore not hypothetical projects or schemes to be followed to the letter; they are descriptions of work actually carried out in schools, intended as models to illustrate ways of thinking about and developing puppetry activities. Each account is in two parts: first, a general description of the activity, then details of ways in which various curriculum areas were involved in the topic. In these latter sections, the possibilities for introducing and developing language in all curriculum areas discussed in Part One, are a basic assumption and will not be reiterated for every topic. It is accepted that such language possibilities are there in all aspects of the work.

Civics project

A few members of a class of seven-year-olds were engaged in improvized puppetry activities. The puppets used were simple rod puppets representing a mother, father, son and daughter and from one or two of their encounters it became clear that the children understood very little about how their local community was organized, how they received their gas, water, electricity, and so on. A general discussion ensued which resulted in different children volunteering to make puppets of different members of the community. A civics project was under way.

Each child made it his or her task to find out about the function of the puppet he had made—the mayor, the housing manager, the town clerk, etc. They conducted their research by consulting books, writing letters and interviewing (with the help of cassette tape recorders) many people in the community, who responded splendidly. The children wrote up their findings and also gave each other brief oral reports. They then improvized various situations with the puppets, making use of this information.

The overall theme was that the family was moving to a new town and therefore had to find a house and a new school for the children. Father and mother were to have interviews for jobs, etc. This led to work in English, maths and environmental studies, and to numerous encounters such as the parents taking the children along to the nearby school to talk to the head teacher and meet the class teacher, the social and emotional value of which will be readily recognized.

Shadow puppets from the civics project

These episodes were based on factual elements and the awareness of the community that they promoted was considerable, but there were also touches of humour, conflict, drama and many insights into the child's view of the world.

Curriculum areas involved

Language: Reading and recording of information; interviewing; writing letters; imaginative stories; writing outlines of encounters; letters to friends at previous school (imaginary).

Mathematics: Plans of town and school; maps and co-ordinates; distances; time—appointments, leaving home, starting school, play times, going home, etc.; money and shopping.

Environmental studies and science: Various aspects of the way the community works; generation of electricity; processing of gas; reservoirs and the purification of water; refuse disposal; visits to a building site—seeing houses in different stages of development, the laying of drains and other facilities, road building; visits to fire and ambulance stations; visit from the police in connection with road safety (some rather gruesome puppets emerged from road safety episodes!); the local shops and street market.

Movement and drama: Improvized encounters and planned scenes of various sorts, giving insights into the running of the community, exploring relationships, e.g. interviews for jobs, visiting the new school, visiting the local Council Housing Department, going to view houses; reactions to the houses and people living in them; reluctance to leave friends.

Craft: Making puppets, props and staging; making a model of the town and of the school; painting, drawing and modelling connected with all aspects of the topic.

The secret of fire

This project was the final term's activity for a class of eleven-year-olds. It was the school custom for the oldest children to present a small performance in the summer term and some suggested a puppet play. The idea met with the unanimous approval of the class and almost all the classwork for the term centred around the project.

The play, *The secret of fire*, was concocted from a mixture of stories written by the children and offered for general consideration. The final form of the story, a scenario, emerged through discussion, written work and improvization with and without puppets. There was no script as such, which kept the performance fresh.

The next stage was the construction of the puppets (marionettes), scenery, props and stage, involving art, crafts of many · sorts and mathematics. Technical problems, such as how to create the illusion of fire and how to get the puppet to pick up a rock and throw it across the stage, provided challenges of a different sort, none of which defeated the children. Constructional methods drew on junk materials on the one hand, and professional joints (using suitable materials with which the children could cope) on the other.

Costume, lighting and sound involved craft activities, colour symbolism, science and music (created by the children). Then there were rehearsals which included the children's own explorations in dramatic encounters, movement, mime, and finally the performance which was a great success. Although there were only eight puppets in the whole story, every child in the class of thirty-five was involved, doing a necessary job—whether manipulating and speaking, looking after props, arranging the scenery, lighting or sound, or handling the stage management.

One child, Mark, who was rather awkward and clumsy and for whom things often went wrong, had taken part in the construction and the preparation of the performance but did not wish to be involved directly in the performance itself. Instead, he asked to show people to their seats, which was also a valued contribution: having somebody to help in this way is all part of the 'theatre experience' and helps proceedings to run smoothly. During the lunch break before the first afternoon's show he went home to get ready and returned transformed, wearing his best trousers and a neatly pressed shirt (which was not usually the case, but Mark had insisted on the shirt being pressed and Mum had eventually given in). He performed his duties well in his own individual manner ('Can I see your invitation please, lady?' his gruff little voice asked. 'Right, come this way please.'). After the show one child commented, to general assent, 'Didn't Mark do his job well?' Mark's face beamed and he grew inches in minutes. He had made his contribution too.

Environmental studies were involved in the project in two ways. First there was the background research for the play, set in ancient Persia: How

A scene from *The Secret of Fire*

did they dress? What did their homes look like? How did they tell the time? (Maths came in here too.) Why did they dress in this way or have that style of building? Why a sand clock rather than a water clock? These were just a few of the many questions to be answered for the play, so the children had considerable experience of seeking and using knowledge for a purpose. During the course of the project one child asked: 'Did the Persians have puppets?' This gave rise to the second environmental studies aspect of the project, *The story of puppets*, discussed later.

Curriculum areas involved

Language: Original stories; précis; ideas to be remembered and tried out; lists of puppets and props and scenery to be made and significant details to be recorded; scenario; prop lists; cues for exits and entrances, curtains, scene changes, sound effects, music and lighting; invitations; programmes; reading and recording of background information.

Mathematics: Size of puppets, proportions of the puppets and their size relative to each other; accurate measurement of puppet parts and staging; measurement and angles for jointing (e.g. knee joints and joining stage parts); rigid structures; plans and elevations; solids and surfaces—nets for constructing shapes for props; patterns and shape (building, decoration, etc. for backcloths, props and puppets); maps, reference points, directions (finding the way to the caves in the mountains and finding the way back); measuring temperature; time—telling the time, the calendar.

Science: Sound effects; lighting and effects; mixing of lights for atmosphere; coloured lighting—how filters work, blending colours, different effects of coloured lighting on different colour costumes; fire and the forging of weapons (linked to the blacksmith, past and present); pulleys, levers and counterweights (curtains and effects).

Environmental studies: Persia in ancient times, homes, ways of life, dress, climate, weapons, etc.

Music: Listening to various pieces of music for ideas for background and atmosphere; creating music with percussion and wind instruments, improvized instruments, string and percussion.

Movement: Exploring encounters in movement and mime; exploring the way different characters would move—tried by the children themselves and with puppets—powerful movements, deliberate movements, gentle, timid movements, etc.; exploring the use of space. The topic also provided many themes for other movement lessons.

Drama: The performance; exploring scenes and possibilities with and without puppets; developing a logical sequence; exploring intentions and consequences, issues concerning the abandoning of a baby (an early incident in the story) and justifications of fighting and warfare; considering how characters of different rank would speak and behave towards each other.

Craft: Making puppets, props and staging. This included woodwork, modelling, junk modelling, gluing, sewing, cutting, making joints of various kinds, handling texture, pattern and colour, using dyes, drawing and painting (for puppet activities and related studies).

The story of puppets

This focus of interest would have been enough for a whole term's work in itself. It led the children to find out about China and India four thousand years ago, Ancient Greece and Rome, the Civil War in England, street entertainments and fairs, Java, Japan, America, Sicily, Austria and Eastern Europe. The story of puppet theatre touches most countries of the world, sometimes preceding the human drama, sometimes reflecting it; its spread and its rises and declines in popularity are related to many religious beliefs, historical factors, geographical features and technological advancements. It is a fascinating story, rich in content for the school curriculum.

Curriculum areas involved

Language: Reading and recording of background information; discussions of why certain types of puppet were likely to have been used and reasons for rises and declines in puppet popularity; discussion of puppets seen and re-telling of stories performed, including sequencing; reading and discussion of traditional puppet plays (e.g. in relation to a specific period: Punch used to be carried off to Hell by the Devil, but in later versions Punch beats the Devil and, later still, the Devil becomes Bogey Man, then Crocodile).

Environmental studies: Touching upon many periods of history and many countries; ritual and religion from early times, religious taboos and

Below left and above: children's paintings from 'the story of puppets'

fertility rites, moving images in the temples; classical times and records of puppetry in Greece and Rome; the collapse of the Roman Empire and spread of wandering entertainers; the Dark Ages; the Italian *Commedia dell' Arte* and Pulcinella, who becomes the French Polichinelle; Civil War in England and the spread of puppetry; Charles II returns bringing Polichinelle, who becomes Punchinello, developing into Punch of the familiar Punch and Judy pair; fashionable puppet shows and Samuel Pepys; influences from abroad; the large travelling shows; development of fairground and pleasure garden entertainment and puppetry for children; twentieth-century puppetry, including cabaret, variety, film and television puppets; parallel development of puppetry through-out eastern and western Europe and the popular folk heroes akin to Punch; puppetry in America—American Indian puppets and the development from the mask to the marionette, the introduction of popular folk heroes of other countries, the influence of immigrant puppeteers and the major developments to the present day; puppetry in Asia—connections with religion, the *Ramayana* and *Mahabharata*, and with the human dance-drama; ways in which early Asian puppetry influenced later developments in the West, and unusual styles of puppet.

Science and Craft: Techniques for making traditional puppets and methods of performing; e.g. lighting, creating shadows, treating leather to make it translucent, then colouring with dyes; modern technology, equipment and materials, and their influence on puppetry; techniques for making animated puppet films, both silhouette and three-dimensional; televi-sion techniques; technical effects; making reproductions of traditional puppets (though it is not usually possible to use the actual materials).

Reading project

The impetus for this activity came from one of my projects which aimed at encouraging children to enjoy books and read for pleasure. The children were first presented with a puppet performance (full-colour shadows) based closely upon the text of an interesting, well illustrated story book. The puppets were translated directly from the illustrations so that the children would later be able to identify the performance with the book. After the performance, the book, which had been shown briefly earlier, was looked at with the children so that they could see that the 'magic' that had been created in the show could be captured in books too.

In the ensuing discussion the children re-told the story, identifying characters and events in the book, and were encouraged to talk about it. A copy of the book was left in the school so that they could re-read it as often as they wished. They were also shown how to make some simple puppets for themselves so that they could present their own stories if they wished.

The children later did make shadow puppets to re-tell stories which they had enjoyed reading and some were presented to other classes. They then built further episodes around the characters in some of the stories. For immigrant children this kind of approach was found to be of particular value. These children were first given a summary of the action they were to see. This was given in their native language (usually Punjabi) so that they could follow the performance in English more easily. They seemed to benefit from the impact made by the performance and the fact that they could then go back over the action in the book as often as they needed, linking the powerful imagery with the written and oral word.

Below left and above: shadow puppets from *Arrow to the Sun*

Curriculum areas involved

Language: Encouragement of children to read stories presented; reading to present their own stories; discussion of what had been seen and sequencing; précis of stories read and discussion of what is the important information to include; writing scenarios for their own plays and lists of puppets, props and scenery required.

Mathematics: Measurement and size of puppets, screen (including size of puppets relative to screen, allowing *space* for action); shapes of puppets and scenery; angles for lighting screen without casting shadows of the puppeteers; time—in the stories—how long the puppet travelled, growing up, etc.; distance.

Environmental studies: Finding out about places in the story presented and for their own plays—Pueblo Indians (and the survival of the North American Indians), Africa, India and the West Indies; not just ways of life but also the different religious beliefs and superstitions which often emerged in folk tales.

Music: Using instruments of different countries, usually brought to the school by the children of immigrant families; making instruments of similar types; creating music for plays—usually fairly simple rhythms (maths was also involved here).

Movement and drama: Enactment of scenes and plays; developing a play, considering how to end it with dramatic impact; consideration of use of space, how the characters move—human and animal; exploring elements of story, e.g. how the boy was treated by the adults from whom he sought help, what the children would do in his position, how the other children in the story behaved, whether they intended harm or mischief or deserved punishment, etc.

Craft: Making shadow puppets and shadow screen; pattern, detail, colour and texture; careful use of scissors.

171

Opposites

The topic began after four five-and-a-half to six-year-old children had read Bears in the Night by S. and J. Berenstain (Collins, 1972); two then used shadows and two used glove puppets to act out the very simple story line which is concerned with '*out* of bed . . . *over* the bridge . . . *around* the lake . . .' etc. A few difficulties were encountered in getting certain types of puppet to perform certain actions but acceptable conventions were developed.

The children then thought of other things the bears might do and, as in the story, reversed the sequence of the actions. They made up short stories and poems using these different concepts and reversals of the action. This led into further discussion of opposites—of size, shape, character, etc. as well as actions.

Puppets were made to illustrate these opposites and the children made up further stories and poems for the puppets to act which included concepts such as taller and shorter, fatter and thinner, wider and narrower, here and there, near and far, towards and away from, over and under, behind and in front of, forwards and backwards, around and through, above and below, in and out. Subsequently concepts such as time and weight were treated similarly.

Curriculum areas involved

Language: Working with the various concepts mentioned above and presenting them in a relevant context; using opposites; exploring stories and poems—both taken from books and made up by the children; sequencing and reversing actions.

Mathematics: Using various mathematical concepts, relating to shape, size, length, height, time, weight, distance; measurement and comparisons; combined concepts—e.g. taller but lighter, shorter but higher, etc.

Music: Linking notes and rhythms to concepts in other areas, including maths, e.g. long and short notes, loud and quiet, high and low, fast and slow rhythms—in keeping with the movement of puppets; the challenging task of creating rhythm and synchronizing this with puppet movement; exploring ways of creating different moods, indicating which puppet is approaching, etc.

Movement and drama: Exploration of various movements and encounters as discussed above.

Craft: Making puppets, by drawing, cutting out, gluing, modelling, sewing, taping, painting, decorating, and exploring pattern, texture and colour.

Reflection and shadows

I was invited to give a brief demonstration of different types of puppet to a class of five-and-a-half to six-year-olds. While looking at a particular rod puppet, one child commented on its eyes; we talked about what they were (shiny silver buttons) and why they made good eyes (because they caught the light and looked as though they were moving as the puppet moved). One little girl could see her face in the buttons and said, 'If you look in my eyes you can see your face too'. So we did just that, and we talked about *reflection*—they had just been polishing up objects with the teacher so it all tied in beautifully. Then we looked for other things that reflected and that could be used for eyes—tin foil, bottle tops, buttons on their clothes. We discussed which would work well, which would not and why not.

Moving on, a little later we came to shadow puppets. First, what is a shadow? When do we see shadows? What makes shadows? We looked at the shadows of objects in the room and at our own shadows, making our shadows move. We then went on to consider shadow puppets themselves, including their size, shape, decoration, texture and colour. During all this, one child observed, 'When you look in the mirror you can see your shadow', just the sort of error from which we can learn about a child's thinking and understanding. It was a delightful comment to take up and explore, helping him, through activity, to understand the difference between a shadow and a reflection. Further work with puppets built upon and reinforced the work on these concepts by providing many different opportunities in which he continued to meet the concepts in meaningful contexts.

Curriculum areas involved

Language: Oral language relating to performance; main points written down by the teacher, read by the children; simple written record linked to pictures, concerned with the story, shadows and reflection; discussion of all these ideas.

Mathematics: Sorting and matching (eyes) and categorizing; counting: comparisons; symmetry linked to reflection; size of puppets, scenery, etc.

Science: Reflection; light and shade, silhouettes, distortion of shadows caused by pulling away from screen, twisting, changing position of source of light, etc.

Movement: Exploring their own shadows and the images they created in sunlight (in the hall), changing shapes of shadows, 'shadowing' each other; exploring reflection, acting as partner's reflection.

Drama: Various brief playlets acted with glove, rod and shadow puppets.

Craft: Making glove, rod and shadow puppets and scenery; using colour, texture, decoration and pattern; symmetry: making 'butterfly' prints of various sorts and folded paper cuts.

Time

The topic arose when a group of ten-year-olds, working on a science topic, encountered the concept of distance measured in light years. Out of the ensuing discussion arose the idea of a time machine and soon puppets were being made to act a basic story-line the children had worked out.

With the time machine the puppets were able to travel through time and space, visiting other ages (past and future) and places, including other planets. Each element of the story led into many avenues of enquiry. Some of the group were still a little unsure of some rather basic notions of the concept of time and, as they were rather slow learners, they tended to focus upon seasons, calendars, simple timetables and the like; others were exploring incidents in history or trying to grasp, for example, just what it must have been like to live in Puritan times. Many also hypothesized about the future and the most able showed their ability to conceive of forms of life

A character from the 'time' project

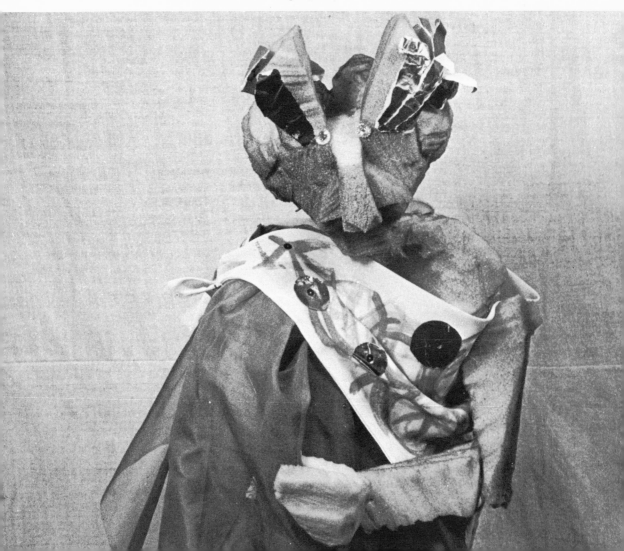

not in terms of human or animal forms but in terms of a force or mass of energy, represented on a shadow screen by simply an intense light or a colour.

Shadow puppets were made to dematerialize (moving them away from the screen, blurring, then fading out the image) and rod puppets and marionettes offered scope for a wide variety of forms. Travelling into the past also led the children to investigate ways in which the time was told in the different ages they visited and one small group produced a very well presented account of time-keeping through the ages, from sundials, water and sand clocks to the first pendulum clock and developments up to the very latest watches. This was not a puppet activity but led directly from one. Another avenue explored related back to the original stimulus—finding out about other planets; this was also developed in ways similar to those discussed a little later under 'Space exploration'. Needless to say the activities involved all kinds of writing: documentation, creative writing, constructing scenarios, etc.

Curriculum areas involved

Language: Reading and recording of information; imaginative story writing; working out scenarios, characters etc. for plays; looking at writing in different periods from copies of original documents (the *Jackdaw* series was useful for this work), deciphering the meaning, looking at the words in relation to words used today.

Mathematics: Distance; time—days, weeks, seasons, calendars; telling the time, timetables and schedules; telling the time in various ways throughout history; speed.

Science: Investigating the planets and the solar system; the formation of planets; measurement of distance in light years.

Environmental studies: Research into various periods and events in history—the Middle Ages, Elizabethan England, Puritan times and the Civil War, the Gunpowder Plot, the Fire of London, the Princes in the Tower, signing of the Magna Carta, the development of clocks and watches, etc.

Music: Finding out about the instruments and music of different periods; listening to recordings of music played on appropriate instruments; making up space age music, experimenting to make different sounds and notes.

Movement and drama: Exploring movement in relation to the music of different periods and the different qualities of movement suggested by different types of music and instruments; acting out encounters in different periods linked with events, characters, ways of life, beliefs and the morality of the age.

Craft: Making puppets—rods, shadows and marionettes—props and scenery; building models, including a time machine; doing drawings and paintings in connection with environmental studies; making different sorts of 'clocks'.

Animals

A student teacher who had been working with a class of seven- and eight-year-olds suggested that they might like to extend the work they had been doing on the animals kept in the school by making puppets of animals and creating a few short performances with them. The idea was enthusiastically received by every child so they set about making all manner of puppets: solid and full-colour shadows, rod puppets, glove puppets (animal heads on a standard glove), sleeve puppets and marionettes made from cartons. These took the form of all manner of animals too, pets, wild animals, prehistoric animals, etc.

Not having anticipated the problem of relative sizes, the student teacher ran into some difficulties, when the puppets were made, in helping the children to form groups and pursue their particular areas of interest, but was alert enough to spot and use this opportunity to look at proportion, relative size, etc. at an appropriate level. Though there was overlap between the areas explored, the groups tended towards areas of special interest, some generally performing animal stories found in books or making up their own. One group focused upon religious studies and the story of Noah, another was attracted by folk tales from Asia, Africa and the West Indies. Some were drawn to find out about animals used for work and transport and the story of *Black Beauty* was brought in. Jungle adventures, zoos and farms proved popular, as did prehistoric animals and finally, a puppet circus presented by shadows and marionettes.

A scene from *Noah*

Curriculum areas involved

Language: Reading and documentation of information; reading and writing animal stories, jungle adventures, etc.; writing précis of action; constructing scenarios for plays.

Mathematics: Shape, size and proportions of puppets; relative sizes; time (e.g. time taken to build the ark, how often to feed pets, etc.).

Science and environmental studies: Animals of all kinds, their habits and habitats, needs for survival; preservation of wild life; morality of the 'law of the jungle'; prehistoric times and development from sea creatures; structure of different animals; man in relation to other animals; process of natural selection; animals native to Britain and those of other countries; animals at work and in war; farms and farm animals, animals bred for food in various countries; visit to zoo; looking after pets.

Music: Various pieces of music connected with animals, including *Peter and the Wolf*; circus music.

Movement and drama: Noah and the Flood; folk stories and other animal stories enacted; episodes improvized to music, especially with shadow puppets. (The circus performance had little dialogue—nearly all the items were set to a background of circus music.)

Craft: Making puppets, props, scenery and staging; paintings, drawings and models connected with background studies; texture in relation to collage pictures of animals and jungle scene.

The development of a city

This topic was distinct from the civics project discussed earlier (see page 163) in that its emphasis was on how towns developed rather than simply how they are organized and managed today. All the classes in the school (five to eleven years of age) were contributing to a project on the City of Plymouth and its relation to how towns developed generally. Various art and craft activities were involved; puppetry was just one, used to depict scenes of everyday life, special events and notable characters from early times to the present day. Information was collected by exploring the local environment, places of interest, museums and libraries, old school log books, conducting 'interviews' and using reference books.

In particular, the work focused on the following: Plymouth and district in early times; its development as a port; Drake and the Spanish Armada; Buckland Abbey (at one time owned by Drake); St Budeaux Church (where Drake was married) and St Budoc, after whom it was named; the Pilgrim Fathers and the sailing of the *Mayflower*; the Citadel (built in the 1660s) by Charles II; the development of the dockyard and naval base; Dartmoor prison (although this was outside the city, the children were keen to include it because of the possibilities for stories and plays); building and engineering achievements like the Brunel Railway Bridge and the Eddystone Lighthouse; Captain Scott's voyage in the *Enterprise* to the South Pole and his fate after the trek to the Pole; the First and Second World Wars and the rebuilding of the modern Plymouth after the Blitz. Most of these events or characters gave rise to puppet activities which did much to reinforce the learning and motivate further investigation.

All this work was considered in relation to the general development of towns from small dwellings and villages, touching on Roman times, Viking raids, the Norman invasion, the development of trade, law and order, the Civil War, travel by road, the development of the railways, social and welfare facilities and amenities generally, education, industry, newspapers, emergency services, local government today and town planning for the future, to mention but a few of the topics covered.

Curriculum areas involved

Language: Interviews, letters, reading and recording of information; stories and plays connected with historical events; the creation of plays from stories; constructing a scenario, etc.

Mathematics: Time; measurement; plans and maps, reference points and directions; shape, size, proportions, etc.

Environmental studies: Many visits in the locality; researching in various ways information concerned with different periods in history.

Crafts: Making puppets of all types; using many art forms to represent historical incidents, geographical features, make rubbings, sketches, paintings, etc.

Adventurers and explorers

This topic was developed by eight- and nine-year-olds. Puppets were introduced to depict real characters and events in their lives, some of which, of necessity, involved a certain amount of conjecture. These adventurers included Columbus, Drake, Gilbert, Grenville, Hawkins, Magellan, Marco Polo, Raleigh, etc.

The work linked with the puppetry included research of factual information (e.g. Drake the pirate, the *Golden Hind*, life on board ship, preserving provisions, engaging in battle, the Spanish Armada), reading fictional stories connected with the period, imaginative work based on fact such as scenes from a battle, mutiny at sea, being press ganged, storm at sea and shipwreck. Maths work, apart from the usual possibilities of handling shape, size, measurement, etc. always present when making puppets, featured distances travelled and time at sea, calculating speed, direction and reference points, reading simple maps, dealing with time in terms of the calendar, keeping a log and planning rations, trading, etc. Considerable work was also done on the places explored, discovered or visited, the inhabitants and their ways of life. By-products of the main theme were the topics 'Smugglers and Pirates' and 'Shipwreck'.

Curriculum areas involved

Language: Reading and recording of information; reading and writing fictional stories and stories based on fact; constructing a scenario, etc.

Mathematics: Shape; size; measurement; distance; maps, directions, co-ordinates, routes; time and speed, calendar (log book); money and trading, tokens, bartering; rations; temperature.

Science and environmental studies: Voyages of exploration; heroes; other countries, climates, ways of life and beliefs; significance of discoveries for colonization, trade, etc.; charting the globe; means of navigation.

Drama: Linked to incidents in history and the performance of some of these; exploring situations such as trying to communicate in other lands, use of gesture, misunderstandings, etc.

Craft: Making rod puppets for action scenes and encounters in 'close-up'; shadow puppets for narrative.

Smugglers and pirates

An off-shoot of the previous topic for those interested was the exploration of the life of smugglers, the revenue men, the 'smuggling run', their ships and routes, tricks at sea and on land to avoid being caught, justice and the penalties imposed. The theme was brought up-to-date with a look at the customs and gave rise to informative and highly amusing encounters acted out with puppets.

The work on pirates obviously overlapped, but also focused upon pirates from classical times (Polycrates; the capture and ransom of Julius Caesar), Vikings, Alfred the Great and the organization of the first English navy to resist pirates, the Middle Ages and the Cinque Ports (and how this led to open piracy), Elizabethan pirates/adventurers and the Spanish Armada, Barbary Corsairs and Christian slaves, the buccaneers of the Caribbean, famous pirates, the Bias Bay incident in 1927, the effect of communications and better policing, and piracy today.

Curriculum areas involved

Language: Reading and documentation of information; reading and creating fictional stories and plays, and others based on fact; constructing a scenario, etc.; *Treasure Island* read with the whole class.

Mathematics: Maps, routes, co-ordinates and directions; tax and duty payable linked to money, measurement and weight; trading; rations; sharing the booty; shapes and angles—sails, masts, rigging; angles of elevation with reference to cannon.

Environmental studies: Historical and geographical aspects of the topics detailed above; customs and policing of national and international waters; the river police; piracy today (e.g. hijacking of airliners).

Music: Sea shanties.

Movement and drama: Various movement themes suggested by the topic; puppet plays concerned with mutiny at sea, press gangs, walking the plank, Bodmin Moor and the Jamaica Inn, episodes from *Treasure Island*; moral issues explored with reference to hijacking to escape oppressive régimes.

Crafts: Puppets, props and scenery; art connected with background studies, models of ships, etc.

Shipwreck

The enactment of a shipwreck, how it happened, scenes of panic on board, picking up survivors and reaching land was presented with considerable intensity. It also gave rise to many other considerations such as the exploration of the island, the possibility of hostile inhabitants, wild animals, the basic needs for survival, the building of shelter, improvized weapons for hunting and tools for building and farming. There was also the possibility of never being found so the children had to consider long-term plans for the development of their island which was a challenging task: what were they going to put on their island, bearing in mind their limited facilities? Where were they going to put it and why? This turned out to be a particularly valuable experience which reflected very clearly the level of cognitive development reached by individual children; some were much more egocentric than others in the sorts of planning that was proposed. It was also interesting to hear the puppets debating the relative merits of different suggestions and the sorts of arguments that were brought to bear on the decision making. Some children who had never shown themselves to be leaders became quite involved and stood their ground, presenting their cases, not dogmatically but sensibly and rationally, and carried others with them by the weight of their arguments.

Curriculum areas involved

Language: Mainly work with fiction—reading and writing; focus on the sounds, atmosphere, panic; poetry; précis; scenario for puppets.

Mathematics: Distance; maps, co-ordinates, longitude and latitude; time-keeping; calendar; weather charts and temperature.

Science and environmental studies: Survival at sea and on land; hunting for food—vegetable and animal; building shelter; floating and sinking; drinking water; creating tools; power; developing an island and its resources; sinking of the *Titanic*.

Music: Instruments improvized from the natural environment to create entertainment.

Drama and movement: Acting out of themes including shipwreck, reaching land, exploration and dangers, electing a leader, division of labour, decision making, extracts from stories, including *Treasure Island*.

Craft: Making puppets, props and scenery; paintings of shipwrecks; making a model of the island, and the developments on it.

Space exploration

A television broadcast for schools provided the impetus for this activity. It had been concerned with the solar system and included models of planets to illustrate certain aspects of the topic. It was obviously not easy to grasp, and perhaps actually animating simpler versions of such models could help to reinforce the concepts. In place of the elaborate mechanical models seen on the screen, therefore, the children made their own planets and quickly moved from exploring their paths in relation to each other (they were mounted on rods painted black) to looking at night and day, the long periods of darkness and light at the Poles, etc.

They soon realized that this exercise could be quite entertaining and began manipulating the planets to music, illuminating them against a black drape in a darkened room. The effect was very powerful and appealing. One day, a few children emerged from a quiet corner where, with permission, they had been putting together a very secret idea of their own. Not even the teacher was allowed to see what was happening until it was ready; it had been rehearsed during a lunch break. This closely guarded secret turned out to be a highly successful 'Dance of the planets' performed to music with full-colour shadow puppets.

As the project developed it encompassed early notions about our own planet and its shape. Glove and rod puppets enacted scenes showing great sailors trying to gather a crew in the face of reluctance caused by fears of sailing over the edge of the world. When they were convinced that it was spherical, they still had to be persuaded that they would not fall off the under-side of the globe, or that the blood would not rush to their heads! Attempts to explore space were also covered, leading up to manned space flight and the landing on the moon. The children reconstructed the interior of a space craft using large cardboard boxes and used this as a booth in which the puppets acted. It was interesting to see that children who were able in mathematics but not generally over-enthusiastic became very involved in calculations of weight, distance, time, fuel, course and directions, angles of entry, etc.

Fictional stories of space exploration were also brought into conjectures about the possibilities of life on other planets, other solar systems, imaginary space creatures, the problems of communication with such creatures, trying to describe our world and our ways of life to them, and creating a city in space as an extension of the sky-lab projects which had placed some of our previous, 'wild' ideas in perspective. As one boy asked: 'When you were a little boy, did you believe men would walk on the moon?'

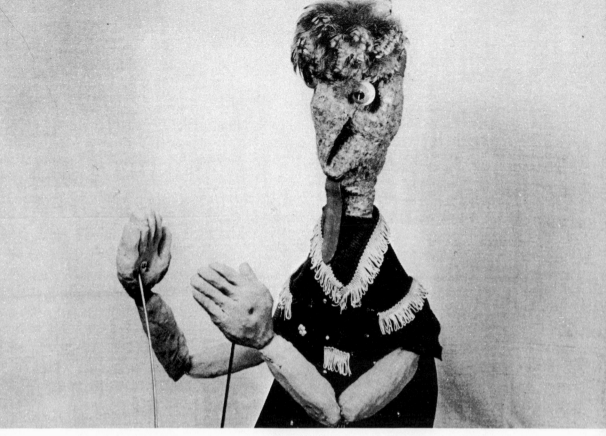

A space creature

Curriculum areas involved

Language: Reading of fiction and non-fiction; writing about space, imaginary creatures and planets, space patrols, rescue missions in space.

Mathematics: Night and day and other concepts of time in relation to the movement of the planets; shapes traced by paths of planets; weight; distance; time; fuel; course and directions; angle of re-entry.

Science and environmental studies: Planets and their formation and movement in space; partial and total eclipses; early notions of the Earth and its shape; gravity; space flight from early rockets and Sputniks up to walking on the Moon and space labs; dangers of re-entry and splash-down; rescue; creating a 'city' in space; likelihood of life on other planets.

Music: Recorded music (e.g. the *Planets Suite*) and music created by the children; experiments to create 'space age' music including improvized instruments, playing tapes at wrong speed or backwards.

Movement and drama: Plays based on fiction and non-fiction; the 'Dance of the planets' referred to above; animation of planets in space; exploring unknown planets, different gravities, weightlessness, disorientation, and related concepts through movement.

Craft: Making planets attached to rods; space craft interior; astronaut puppets and creatures from other planets; models of surface of the Moon, space craft and lunar modules.

Spies and spying

This work with twelve-year-olds arose from a boy's story about Dick Barton, inspired by the television series. Various areas were developed covering aspects of history and geography, science, science fiction, extensive written language, the mathematics of time, distance, codes and equations, logical deduction, etc. The children read widely—both fiction and non-fiction—and there were many instances of language which they had met in their reading then being used in playlets with puppets (*secretive, furtive, stealthily, etc.*).

The boy initially wanted to present his story with puppets and did so, but the work went beyond puppets alone and the children devised problems which had to be solved by logical deduction, after the fashion of the *Masterspy* television programme, challenging each other with them. (In many ways devising the problems was more challenging than solving them.) Some of these problems were used in the puppet activities to test suspects who were being interrogated. Needless to say, there were some bloodthirsty torture scenes but it is interesting that, after the initial surge of fictional exploits, what really captured their enthusiasm was stories of real spies and the spying techniques employed today.

While the project was developing, the press was giving wide coverage to claims that an assassination squad was operating against certain political defectors in Western Europe. The newspapers were scoured daily for more information about the killing of Georgi Markov by means of a poisoned umbrella tip in a London street. A careful record was kept marked, not by any unpleasant inquisitiveness but by a sensitive understanding of the real human element in what had seemed previously to be a glamorous profession. The work also opened up in another direction to include criminal detection and undercover police work, also represented through puppet encounters and recorded in writing. For most of the activity rod puppets were used, with occasional shadow puppet stories, solid black shadows silhouetted on a white screen coming across particularly well for scenes of suspense. The work fell into three main areas:

Fictional special agents: James Bond, Dick Barton, etc.—items based on books and children's own ideas based on these characters, the puppets giving scope for special effects, fantasy and the amazing physical abilities of their heroes.

True stories of spies: Improvization of encounters at different periods in history—e.g. King Alfred, 'Cicero' (the German spy Bazna), Richard Sorge (the Russian master spy), Commander Crabbe (including possible explanations of his disappearance) and famous women spies such as Mata Hari, the Cat and Odette Sansom.

Spying techniques: Codes and breaking codes, ways of passing messages, disguises, interrogation, spy planes and satellites, counter-intelligence, criminal intelligence and undercover police work.

Curriculum areas involved

Language: Reading and documentation of background information; reading and writing of fiction; discussion of stories read, films seen, with emphasis on sequence, accurate description, important points; constructing scenario, etc. for puppet encounters.

Mathematics: Codes and equations; breaking codes and solving equations; logical puzzles; time; distance; speed on land and at sea; magnification (multiplication).

Science and environmental studies: Spies throughout history and their exploits; spying techniques, old and modern; police undercover work; military intelligence; industrial spies; links with assassination and terrorism; photography and telephoto lenses, binoculars, periscopes, focal lengths; signalling with lights and mirrors (including angles of incidence and reflection) and buzzers (morse keys, experimenting with electric bells); firing at underwater targets (refraction).

Music: Creating and listening to (and discussing) music with atmosphere—sinister, eerie, tense, menacing, etc.

Movement and drama: Movement themes taken from stories and music; disguises and moving in character; plays based on real and fictitious incidents.

Craft: Making puppets, props and scenery, illustrations for background studies, making a periscope, simple camera (pin-hole camera) and other equipment such as morse buzzer.

Part five
PUPPETRY RESOURCES

Puppetry organizations and centres of activity

Britain:
The Puppet Centre Trust

This body is the national reference and consultancy point for puppet theatre in Britain. It includes an Education and Therapy Unit (originally the Educational Puppetry Association) and combines a research and development function with the co-ordination of information. A registered charity, the Trust is an independent organization housed within the Battersea Arts Centre which has a 120-seat theatre with occasional puppet performances. The Trust offers:

An information and advisory service
A register of professional puppeteers, craftsmen, workshop leaders and lecturers
An extensive reference library of over 1,000 titles
A small display of craftsman-made demonstration and practice figures
Modest workshop facilities and rehearsal space
A sales service for books, leaflets and other materials
Regular (Wednesday and Thursday) evening courses in term time
Termly weekend courses for teachers and others
Monthly family workshops
Occasional master classes and seminars
Lecture-demonstrations and workshops as required.

A puppetry resource room for teachers and pupils is being developed within the Inner London Education Authority's Drama and Tape Centre, Princeton Street, London WC1.

The Trust's publications include:

Animations, a review of puppetry and related theatre, six issues per year, available on subscription
A Directory of Professional Puppeteers (illustrated)
Puppet Post, a termly publication of articles on education and therapy*
How to run a puppet workshop, a book for teachers, playgroup leaders, etc.
Puppets and Therapy, vols I-III, booklets on puppetry in special education and therapy in the widest sense*
Information leaflets on various aspects of puppetry*

* Originally Educational Puppetry Association publications.

The Puppet Centre is open to visitors from 2–6pm (Mon–Fri), at other times by appointment or when events are scheduled. Groups of visitors should book in advance. Enquiries (always enclose an s.a.e.) to:

The Puppet Centre Trust
Battersea Arts Centre
Lavender Hill
London SW11 5TJ   *Telephone*: 01 228 5335

Other centres of activity in Britain

Arts centres throughout the country include puppetry activities from time to time. Those known to be among the most active are included in the list below. For further information about a particular area, contact the local or regional arts centre or association; the Puppet Centre will help if it can but it relies upon other centres to keep it informed.

The Brewery Puppet Centre
Brewery Arts Centre
Kendal
Cumbria   *Telephone*: 0539 25133
A newly developing, very active centre with workshops and performances.

Cannon Hill Puppet Theatre
Midlands Arts Centre for Young People
Cannon Hill Park
Birmingham 12   *Telephone*: 021 440 4221
Regular daily performances in a 200-seat theatre; lecture-demonstrations, courses for teachers, workshops for children, professional training.

Caricature Theatre
Station Terrace
Cardiff CF1 4EY   *Telephone*: 0222 29163
Currently developing new headquarters with many facilities of all types— a five-year project.

Darlington Puppet Centre
Darlington Arts Centre
Vane Terrace
Darlington DL3 7AX   *Telephone*: 0325 483271
A newly established puppet centre, the development of which includes workshops for children, a library and performances at the centre, in the town and in local schools.

Da Silva Puppet Theatre
St James'
Whitefriars
Norwich   *Telephone*: 0603 615564
A new development incorporating a theatre, workshops, a travelling workshop, courses for teachers, etc.

Glasgow Arts Centre
12 Washington Street
Glasgow   *Telephone*: 041 221 4526
Has a resident puppeteer and workshops for children and adults.

Harlequin Puppet Theatre
Cayley Promenade
Rhos-on-Sea
Colwyn Bay
Wales   *Telephone*: (Christopher Somerville) 0492 82062
Open in summer season, includes a summer school and private tuition available throughout the year.

Hayward Marionettes
Abbots Bromley,
Staffordshire
Enquiries: D. Hayward
Edinburgh House
Bagot Street
Abbots Bromley
Nr Rugeley
Staffordshire

A 50-seat theatre taking block bookings only for Thursday evening performances; director is Regional Organiser for the Duke of Edinburgh Award Scheme and will advise on including puppetry in work for an award.

Hogarth Puppets
The White Barn
Whimple
Devon   *Telephone*: 0404 822 107
Major internationally known and respected puppet company with one of the best private collections in the world: two exhibitions—the Hogarth Puppets and an historical collection—available for tour. Always at least one exhibition for viewing. *Visitors by appointment only*.

Little Angel Marionette Theatre
14 Dagmar Passage
Cross Street
London N1   *Telephone*: 01 226 1787
A leading British company with a 100-seat theatre; performances at weekends for young children (Saturday mornings) and older children and adults (Saturday and Sunday afternoons); frequently has weekday performances during school half-terms and holidays and at certain times of the year. All types of puppetry presented, and seasons with guest companies, British and foreign.

The Little Puppet Theatre
Vicarage Road
St Agnes
Cornwall   *Telephone*: 087 255 2154
120-seat theatre with a summer season; facilities include workshop sessions
and lecture-demonstrations and the development of a small studio is
planned. The theatre is developing as a centre for other arts too.

POLKA Children's Theatre
240 The Broadway
Wimbledon   *Telephone*: 01 542 4258
London SW19   *Box Office*: 01 543 0363
Exciting new development by a leading British company, including a 300-
seat theatre, attractively displayed exhibition, workshop for courses,
adventure room, full facilities for the handicapped.

Australia

Puppetry in Australia is developing rapidly but, as yet, there are few
permanent puppet theatre buildings or puppet centres. However, the
following list contains a selection of puppeteers, companies and centres,
through which contact with puppetry activities may be made. See also
'Membership organisations' (pages 192–194) for details of the Puppetry
Guild of Australia and the Australian Centre of the *Union Internationale de la
Marionnette*.

Richard Bradshaw
19 Balfour Road
Kensington
New South Wales 2033
A qualified teacher and professional puppeteer, internationally acclaimed
for his shadow puppetry.

Carelew Arts Centre
11 Jeffcett Street
North Adelaide
South Australia 5006
Tutor in puppetry: Joseph Neevey

Clovelly Puppet Theatre
Director: Edith Murray
'Moonahwarra'
Larson Road
Springwood
New South Wales 2777
A centre now run by the Creative Leisure Movement; the theatre offers
performances and workshops. It has been the introduction to puppet
theatre for a number of established puppeteers.

The Gardner Puppet Company
Director: Laurie Gardner
72 Heathwood Street
East Ringwood
Melbourne
Victoria 3135
Specializes in workshops with an educational emphasis.

Norman Hetherington Puppets
17 Sirius Cove Road
Mosman
New South Wales 2088
Originally a cartoonist, Norman Hetherington is a solo performer with considerable experience of puppetry in television. He is President of the Puppetry Guild of Australia and Chairman of the Australian Centre of UNIMA.

Mrs Rose Hill
c/o PO Mildura West
Victoria 3500
Considerable experience in running workshops.

Mrs Kath Hughes
Mt. Gravatt College of Advanced Education
Messines Ridge Road
Mt. Gravatt
Brisbane
Queensland 4053
A college lecturer with considerable experience of puppetry in education. Kath Hughes is President of the Queensland Puppetry Guild.

Marionette Theatre of Australia
Head Office: 153 Dowling Street
Potts Point
New South Wales 2011
Formed in 1965 as part of the Australian Elizabethan Theatre Trust, it became an independent organization in 1979.

The Nutshell Puppet Theatre
Director: Mrs Nancy Johnson
54 Ord Street
West Perth
Western Australia 6007
Established in 1971, the theatre includes a 50-seat theatre, library, workshop, etc. Nancy Johnson has experience as a lecturer training pre-school teachers.

The Parry-Marshall Puppet Theatre
77 Bowen Street
Camberwell
Victoria 3124
Usually two-person performances, including for schools.

Pocket People Puppet Theatre
Director: Anne Heitmann
PO Box 397, GPO
Adelaide
South Australia 5001
Anne Heitmann, a professional puppeteer, was originally a teacher.

Tasmanian Puppet Theatre
Director: Peter Wilson
PO Box 828H, GPO
Hobart 7001
Formed in 1969, the theatre has developed into one of the major Australian companies.

The United States

In the United States there are many centres which incorporate puppetry activities, including a substantial number of university departments offering various courses in aspects of puppet theatre. These, however, are not 'centres' in the sense intended here (i.e. open to the public for information, etc.) The Puppeteers of America (see Membership Organizations) will be helpful in recommending regional guilds, centres and courses. Those listed below are all fairly recently established and still developing. Each is headed by a leading figure in American puppet theatre but, as is to be expected, every centre has its own personality and emphasis. (At the time of writing the Golden West College in South California was also planning a puppet centre which promised to be worthy of note.)

The Center for Puppetry Arts
1404 Spring Street
Atlanta
Georgia
Offers performances, a workshop and conference areas and a display of some important exhibits.

The Educational Puppetry Resource Center
294 29th Street
San Francisco
California 94131
Offers consultancy programmes, puppetry library, occasional workshops, displays, audio-visual kits and a Resource Guide. Publishes *Puppetry in Education News*.

The National Puppet Center
815 1/2 King Street
Alexandria
Virginia 22314   (Washington DC, Metropolitan area)
Is developing facilities for the performance and study of puppetry in a
converted old vaudeville/movie house.

The National Puppetry Institute
Box U-127 P
The University of Connecticut
Storrs
Connecticut 06268
An independent body housed within the university; a centre for research
and development in puppetry, is building up facilities for professional and
para-professional puppeteers, for the investigation of the social role of
puppetry as an entertainment, as an educational aid and for therapy'.

Membership organizations

Union Internationale de la Marionnette (UNIMA)

An organization with sections or centres in over fifty countries, which seeks
to 'unite the puppeteers of the world'. Activities and facilities include:
    Regular bulletins
    Contacts and information for members travelling abroad
    Information of international puppetry affairs, events, conferences and
    festivals
    A major International Congress and Festival every four years
    Members' meetings
Enquiries to:

Britain:
    Mr T. E. Howard
    5 Greystoke Gardens
    Enfield
    Middlesex
USA:
    Mrs Allelu Kurten
    Browning Road
    Hyde Park
    NY 12538

Australia:
    Mr Norman Hetherington
    17 Sirius Cove Road
    Mosman 2088
Canada:
    Mrs Pat Overgaard
    887 Keith Road
    Vancouver BC

Other Countries:
    For details contact the International Secretariat
    32 Rue Jagiellonska, Apt. 5
    03—719, Warsaw, Poland
    or The Puppet Centre in London (See pages 186–187)

The British Puppet and Model Theatre Guild

The oldest existing puppetry organization in the world, the Guild has regional representatives who help to co-ordinate activities and facilitate contact in different parts of the country. Activities and facilities include:
  Members' meetings
  Occasional exhibitions and festivals
  A monthly newsletter
  A sales section
  The Puppet Master, an occasional journal
Enquiries to:
  Mr Gordon Shapley
  Hon. Secretary/Treasurer
  18 Maple road
  Yeading
  Nr Hayes
  Middlesex

The Puppeteers of America

A national, non-profit organization with members in many countries, established in 1937, which aims to improve the art of puppetry through: educational programmes, annual conferences, workshops, exhibitions, regional and local events, publications, advisory services and sales service of books and related material.

Official Publication:	*The Puppetry Journal* (six issues per year)
National Festival:	Held annually at a different venue each year
Regional Guilds:	Affiliated with the P. of A. and hold monthly meetings
General Enquiries to:	Executive Director: Nancy L. Staub 2311 Connecticut Avenue, Apartment 501 Washington, DC 20008 (202) 265–6564
Membership Enquiries:	Gayle G. Schluter 5 Cricklewood Path Pasadena California 91107

The Puppetry Guild of Australia

An organization with separately administered sections in different areas. Each organises its own activities, including festivals, performances, lectures, demonstrations, films and meetings, and facilitates contact and advice.

For information on the Guild and details of current officers in regional sections, contact:

Norman Hetherington, President
17 Sirius Cove Road
Mosman
New South Wales 2088

Museum Collections

Britain

London:
Bethnal Green Museum of Childhood
Cambridge Heath Road
London E2
Extensive collection including puppets of all types, dolls and toys

Horniman Museum and Library
London Road
Forest Hill
London SE23
Small collection of English, Belgian, African and Asian puppets and theatrical masks from all over the world

The Museum of London
150 London Wall
London EC2
Very little on show but significant collection in store; can be viewed by arrangement

The Museum of Mankind
(The British Museum Department of Ethnography)
6 Burlington Gardens
Piccadilly
London W1
The Raffles Collection of Javanese puppets and a selection of Chinese puppets. The collection is so large that very little is displayed at any one time but other items can be inspected by arrangement.

POLKA Children's Theatre
240 The Broadway
Wimbledon
London SW19
A new theatre with a varied and very well displayed collection.

Pollock's Toy Museum
1 Scala Street
London W1
Toy theatres, puppets and toys

Victoria and Albert Museum
South Kensington
London SW7
Mainly Indian and Indonesian puppets, also toy theatres. Much of the V and A collection is displayed at the Bethnal Green Museum and other items in store can be viewed by arrangement.

Derby:
Derby Museum and Art Gallery
The Strand
Derby
International collection of toy theatres, printed sheets, etc.

Edinburgh:
The Museum of Childhood
34 High Street
Edinburgh
A small but growing collection of exhibits

Liverpool:
Merseyside County Museums
William Brown Street
Liverpool
Collection of Javanese shadows

Oxford:
Pitt Rivers Museum
University of Oxford
Parks Road
Oxford
Mainly shadow figures

Rottingdean:
National Toy Museum
Rottingdean Grange
Rottingdean
Brighton
Small but growing collection

Sunderland:
    Sunderland Music Hall Museum
    Gordon Place
    Sunderland
Modest collection of Victorian puppets

Canada

B. Columbia:
    Centennial Museum
    Vancouver
American north west coast and Javanese puppets

    University of British Columbia Museum
Kwakiutl puppets

Montreal:
    McGill University
Collection of puppets, books and toy theatres

Ontario:
    Royal Ontario Museum of Archaeology
North west coast puppets and marionettes

The United States

California:
    Santa Barbara Museum of Art
A modest collection

    University College of Los Angeles
    (Ethnomusicology, ethnic and theatre collections)
Wide range of puppets from all over the world and some important
American exhibits

Connecticut:
    University of Connecticut
    Storrs
Developing a puppetry centre

Illinois:
    Field Museum
    Chicago
Includes a range of various Asian shadow and rod puppets

Michigan:
    Detroit Institute of Art
Extensive collection, including many items from the Paul McPharlin
Collection, extensive library, photographs and archive material

New Jersey:
  Institute for Advanced Study, Princeton:
  Gest Oriental Library
Over 2500 Chinese shadow exhibits

  Newark Museum
Selection of Asian, Sicilian and Tony Sarg puppets

New Mexico:
  Santa Fe Museum of Arts
Collection of marionettes by Gustave Bauman

  International Folk Art Museum
  Santa Fe
Modest variety of puppet exhibits

  University of New Mexico
  Albuquerque
Selection of puppets from McPharlin Collection, also books and masks

New York:
  Museum of the City of New York

  Brooklyn Museum
Selection of Asian figures plus a few other interesting exhibits

  Cooper Union Museum (now part of the Smithsonian Institute)
A few particularly interesting French and Italian 18th century exhibits

  American Museum of Natural History
Large collection of Asian and American Northwest Coast puppets

Ohio:
  Cleveland Museum of Art
Modest collection of Asian figures

Pennsylvania:
  Mercer Museum
  Doylestown
Sicilian and Chinese puppets and a set of Punch glove puppets

  University Museum
  University of Pennsylvania
Reasonable collection, particularly of Javanese shadows and rod puppets

Virginia:
  University of Richmond
Caroline Lutz collection, with Japanese, Chinese and Mexican exhibits

Washington DC:
  United States National Museum
  Smithsonian Institute
Includes a variety of American Indian, Hawaiian and Asian puppets

Important collections in other countries

Austria:
    Theatre Museum
    National Library of Austria (Vienna)
Richard Teschner's puppets and *Figurenspiegel* theatre

Belgium:
    Theatre Toone
    Place de la Chapelle
    Brussels
Traditional folk puppet theatre with a collection of old puppets

Czechoslovakia:
    International Museum of Marionettes
    Chrudim
The official museum, library and archives of UNIMA

France:
    Musée Internationale de la Marionnette
    Lyons

    Musée de l'Homme
    Paris

Germany:
    Theatre· Museum
    University of Cologne
Over 1500 exhibits

    Puppentheatersammlung der Stadt München
Largest and finest puppet museum in the world

    Deutches Ledermuseum
    Offenbach-am-Maim
Contains large collections of shadow puppets

    Abteilung Puppentheatersammlung
    Dresden
Fine collection of puppets and related material from all over the world

USSR:
    City Museum of Theatre Arts
    Kiev
18th and 19th-century puppet theatres, particularly from the Ukraine

    National Ethnographic Museum of Leningrad
A theatre museum with a selection of interesting puppetry exhibits

    State Central Puppet Theatre
    Moscow
The major puppet theatre in the world, with its own collection of exhibits

Films and Distributors in Britain and North America

Unless otherwise stated, the films listed are available in 16mm colour with sound.

Distributors

The key at the side is used to identify the distributor for each film listed.

ACI   ACI Media, 35 west 45th Street, New York, NY 10036

BGF   Baylis Glascock Films, 1017 N. La Cienega Blvd., Suite 305, Los Angeles, CA 90069

BFI   British Film Institute, Distribution Library, 127 Charing Cross Road, London WC2H OLA

CEA   Carmen Educational Associates Box 205, Youngstown, New York, NY 14174 *and* Pine Grove, Ontario, LOJ 1JO

CWM   Center for World Music, 397 Gravatt Drive, Berkeley, CA 94705

COI   Central Office of Information, Government Buildings, Bromyard Avenue, London W3

CCM   CCM Films, 866 Third Avenue, New York, NY 10022

CFC   Concord Films Council, 201 Felixstowe Road, Nacton, Ipswich IP3 9BJ

CIF   Coronet Instructional Films, 65 East South Water Street, Chicago, IL 60601

CFL   Contemporary Films Ltd., 55 Greek Street, London W1

ETV   Educational and Television Films Ltd., 247a Upper Street, London N1 1RV

EBE   Encyclopaedia Britannica Educational Corporation, Chicago, IL 60611

FI   French Institute, London (Services du Cinéma, L'Institut Français du Royaume Uni), Queensbury Place, South Kensington, London SW7

IFB   International Film Bureau, Inc., 332 South Michigan Avenue, Chicago, IL 60604

JIC   Japan Information Centre, Embassy of Japan, Film Library, 5 Grosvenor Square, London W1X 9LB

JC   Japanese Consulate, San Francisco, California

MGH   McGraw Hill Book Company, Audio-Visual Department, 1221 Avenue of the Americas, New York, NY 10020

NFBC   National Film Board of Canada, 1 Grosvenor Square, London W1X OAB

NYU   NYU Film Library, 26 Washington Place, New York, NY 10003

PF   Phoenix Films, 470 Park Avenue South, New York,
NY 100 16

POA   Puppeteers of America, Audio-Visual Library,
1441 15th Street, Los Osos, CA93402.
(Available to P. of A. members)

SEF   Sterling Educational Films, 241 East 34th Street, New York,
NY 100 16

General films

	Distributor
Acte Sans Paroles (Act without words)	BFI, FI
Puppet version of Beckett's first mime play (11 min)	
Blue Like an Orange	COI, MGH
UNESCO film about puppets all over the world	
Bread and Puppets	NYU
Bunraku	JIC
All aspects of Bunraku puppet theatre	
Bunraku Puppet Theatre of Japan (26 min)	JC
Children's Puppet Theatre	ETV
Puppet theatre at Verna, Bulgaria (15 min)	
Czech Puppets	ETV
History of Czech puppetry, University of Puppetry, Black Theatre performance, historical material and excerpt from Trnka's last film (18 min)	
Dimanche de Gazouilly	FI
A little bird and his companions on their way to a picnic (no commentary) (14 min)	
Kaguya Hime (Princess of the Moon) (15 min)	JC
Legend of the Magic Knives (11 min)	EBE
Marionettes	BFI
Ambitious amateur film about a puppet master who falls in love with one of his creations (B/W, *Silent*, 21 min)	
Marionettes, Construction and Manipulation (10 min)	CCM
The Mascot	BFI
Adventures of a small dog as he attempts to obtain an orange for a sick little girl (*B/W*, 18 min)	
Noman Puppeteers	CFC
Ancient tradition of the string puppets of Rajasthan, India. Outstanding photography (20 min)	
The Orator	CFC
The man who carefully prepares his speech but sends his audience to sleep (10 min)	
Owl and the Raven (8 min)	ACI

The Paper Kite   CFC
> UNICEF film: Norwegian puppet story of a boy who dreams that he visits other countries (20 min)

Puppet Magic   IFB
> Short history of puppetry followed by an introduction to the puppeteer making and manipulating marionettes (12 min)

Puppet on a String (B/W)   COI

Puppetry—String Marionettes (B/W, 11 min)   EBE

Puppets (Spanish) (15 min)   ACI

Puppets You Can Make (16 min)   CIF

Rakvickarma (Coffin Makers)   CFC
> Award-winning, Czech film about two puppets who quarrel, then break each other into pieces (B/W, 10 min)

Robinson's Island (16 min)   ACI

Shadowland (B/W, 12 min)   CCM

The Shadow Puppet Theatre of Java (*Wayang Kulit*)   CWM
> Featuring the puppeteer Oemartopo (22 min)

Shadows, Shadows Everywhere (11 min)   CIF

The Toymaker   CFC
> Two puppets fight because they are different but come to realise that they cannot do without each other (15 min)

Wayang Kulit   CWM
> Malaysian shadow play performed in villages (15 min)

What Hands Can Do (10 min)   SEF

Un touriste en France   FI
> About a tourist in France with his motor car. No commentary (12 min)

Stop-action films

Flight to Venus   BFI
> Award-winning amateur film: plasticine puppets in a space fantasy (11 min))

The Invisible Actor   ETV
> Analysis of making a film by stop-action technique; Czech film, French commentary, English sub-titles (14 min)

L'Idée (The Idea)   BFI
> Based on a book of woodcuts, animated cut-out figures depict the creation and progress of an artistic idea (B/W, 27 min)

Little Umbrella   CFL, MGH
> An old man flies into a nursery on an umbrella and brings the toys to life to put on a show (16 min)

Stop-action films: Jiří Trnka

Arie Prerie (Song of the Prairies)   BFI, CFL
   Parody of the Western (21 min)
The Hand   CFL, CFC,
   Parable on the position of art in the socialist   MGH
   state (25 min)
Jiří Trnka   ETV
   How he created *The Child and His World* (10 min)
Jiří Trnka's Puppets   CFL, MGH
   A visit to his studios, including extracts from his films (18
   min)
A Mid-Summer Night's Dream   CFL, MGH
   Shakespeare's comedy: a masterpiece of puppet animated
   film (74 min)
Puppets of Jiří Trnka (26 min)   PF

Stop-action films: Lotte Reiniger (silhouettes)

The Adventures of Prince Achmed (1923—36)   CFL, CEA
   The first full-length animated feature film in the history of
   the cinema: outstanding. Story taken from the Arabian
   Nights. Original silent titles but with added musical
   score. Available in colour or black and white (65 min)
The Art of Lotte Reiniger   CFL, CEA
   At work on her films. Colour or B/W (12 min)
Aucassin and Nicolette   NFBC
Carmen   CFL, CEA
   Based on themes from Bizet's *Carmen*, ending with humor-
   ous bullfight. No dialogue (B/W, 10 min)
Dr Doolittle (B/W)   CFL, CEA
   Three tales of exploration based on these famous stories
   either as a single film (Silent, 25 min)or as three separate
   films:
       In Darkest Africa (Sound, 10 min)
       In Cannibal Land (Sound, 10 min)
       The Lion's Den (Sound, 10 min)
Galathea   CFL, CEA
   A nude statue comes to life in classical Athens, driving
   men frantic and women mad. No dialogue. (B/W, 12 min)
Harlequin   CFL, CEA
   Amorous adventures of a casanova Harlequin set to 17th-
   century music; no dialogue (B/W, 24 min)
Jack and the Beanstalk   CFL, CEA
   Traditional version (20 min)

Papageno CFL, CEA,
  The Bird Catcher from Mozart's *Magic Flute*. BFI
  No dialogue (B/W, 12 min)
The Star of Bethlehem CFL, CEA
  Nativity play performed as a Medieval Miracle Play
  (Colour, 10 min; B/W, 20 min)
The Stolen Heart CFL, CEA
  German peasants' music making is interfered with by an
  evil wizard. No dialogue (B/W, 10 min)
Other films by Lotte Reiniger: 10 minutes each CFL, CEA
  *Aladdin, Caliph Stork, Cinderella, The Frog Prince, Gallant
  little Tailor, Grasshopper and the Ant, Hansel and Gretel, Little
  Chimney Sweep, The Magic Horse, Puss in Boots, Sleeping
  Beauty, Snow White and Rose Red, The Three Wishes,
  Thumbellina*

Films with foreign dialogue

Aventures de Patatras (a puppet dog) French (18 min) FI No.C/26
Carrousel Boréal (teddy bears) French (10 min) FI No.C/1
Fables of La Fontaine illustrated with glove puppets
1 *Le Lion amoureux*
   La Cour de Lion French (11 min) FI No.C/5
2 *Le Chat, La Belette et le Petit Lapin*
   Le Sevetier et le Financier French (10 min) FI No.C/6
3 *Le Lièvre et la Tortue*
   Le Coche et la Mouche
   La Tortue, la Gazelle, le Corbeau et le Rat French (10 min) FI No.C/7
4 *Le Rat des Villes et le Rat des Champs*
   Le Corbeau et le Renard
   Le Renard et la Cigogne French (10 min) FI No.C/8
5 *La Laitière et le Pot au Lait*
   Le Lion et la Rat
   La Cigale et la Fourmi French (10 min) FI No.C/9
On a volé la mer French (33 min) FI No.C/45
  Featuring the puppets of Yves Joly
Le pauvre matelot French (18 min) FI
  Based on a Jean Cocteau story
Puppet Master Russian (8 min) BFI
  USSR, 1937; film made by the leading Russian puppeteer
  Sergei Obraztsov. *No sub-titles;* B/W

Wood sizes and metrication

The dimensions of timber and dowelling used in the construction of puppets, stages and props have been given in both imperial and metric measures. Though sold in metric lengths, shops still quote widths and thicknesses in both measures.

It must be remembered that the standard widths and thicknesses of wood, quoted throughout this book and in shops, are by convention the sizes of the wood unplaned. The actual dimensions of the wood as sold (i.e. planed) will usually be at least $\frac{1}{8}$th in (3.2mm) under the quoted dimensions.

The equivalent imperial and metric measures for the timber and dowelling referred to in the book are:

Imperial	*Metric*
1×1 in	25×25 mm (sometimes 25.4×25.4 mm)
$1\frac{1}{2} \times 1\frac{1}{2}$ in	38×38 mm
2×2 in	50×50 mm
$\frac{3}{8}$ in diameter	9 mm diameter
$\frac{1}{2}$ in diameter	12 mm diameter

If one needs to convert lengths into metric measures, calculating 25 mm to the inch gives sufficiently accurate results.

Index

Index by Ann Edwards